Losing Alicia

A Father's Journey After 9/11

By John L. Titus

Published by:

FriesenPress

Suite 300 – 852 Fort Street
Victoria, BC, Canada V8W 1H8

www.friesenpress.com

Distributed to the trade by The Ingram Book Company

Table of Contents

Foreword vii

Acknowledgements x

About the Cover xi

Introduction..I

Chapter 1: *Loss and Grief, Politics and Religion* 3

Chapter 2: *The Day That Forever Changed My Life* 17

Chapter 3: *The Journey Begins: An Inside Look at Grief* 23

Chapter 4: *A Prayer and a Vision* 25

Chapter 5: *The Nightmare Continues* 29

Chapter 6: *From Whence Comes the Strength to Go On?* 33

Chapter 7: *Honoring Alicia's Life* 35

Chapter 8: *The Mourning After* 43

Chapter 9: *Grief is a Desolate Journey* 45

Chapter 10: *Amazing Grace* 51

Chapter 11: *San Francisco and Alicia's Apartment* 55

Chapter 12: *Ground Zero* 61

Chapter 13: *Depression, Loneliness, and Despair* 67

Chapter 14: *Good, Evil, and the Political Quagmire* 71

Chapter 15: *Alicia and Divine Presence* 77

Chapter 16: *Peacemaking in a Troubled World* 81

Chapter 17: *The Dawning of a New Day* 83

Chapter 18: *Happiness Is...* 87

Chapter 19: *And Time Goes On* 89

Chapter 20: *Day by Day* 97

Chapter 21: *Running Alicia's Marathon* 101

Chapter 22: *The Joy of Travel and the Mire of Politics* 109

Chapter 23: *Grief Knows No Bounds* 123

Chapter 24: *An Eye for an Eye* 127

Chapter 25: *Not in my Daughter's Name!* 131

Chapter 26: *Ten Years Afterward* 133

Chapter 27: *The Return of Joy* 141

Chapter 28: *"Be the Change"* 145

Chapter 29: *Culpability and the Victim's Compensation Fund* .. 149

Epilogue: *Osama bin Laden is Dead:
the Cycle of Violence Continues* 153

Postscript: *Peace Activities and Events after 9/11* 155

References 158

About the Author 159

Foreword

Of all the tragic deaths, there can be none more excruciating than a parent's loss of a child.

In Losing Alicia, readers not only witness a father's struggle over the murder of his young, vibrant and beautiful daughter, but they walk with him through his agonizing grief after one of the most horrific tragedies in history, September 11, 2001.

Alicia was a flight attendant aboard United Airlines Flight #175, which was the second plane to hit the World Trade Center.

Titus was on his way to work when the first plane struck the North Tower. He saw the second plane on television in real time.

This heart-felt book is the extraordinary story of an extraordinary man dealing with extraordinary circumstances.

As our nation observes the tenth anniversary of 9/11, Titus offers a side of the tragedy too often missed or forgotten after the rush to war, patriotism and national security consumed the country, as this excerpt from his book shows.

"As Bev and I sat down on the precipice in solemn meditation, I prayed that God would come into our hearts. I prayed for understanding and love. I prayed for Alicia's soul and the souls of the others who had died with her earlier in the day. I prayed for our world." Americans as a whole have not dealt with 9/11 let alone made sense of it. However, John Titus has.

A counselor by training, Titus pursues an alternative course rather than join the noisy gongs of war, hatred, fear, vengeance and conspiracy. He dares to address and articulate his strong and conflicting emotions and later, to share them with others in this book. This is an act of courage, faith and love that comes from the conviction that the evils foisted on America and the world on 9/11 not be repeated.

"The only way to deal with grief is to go through its very heart to feel the painful feelings; to cry the tears of sadness; to relive those precious moments of bygone days, now mired in pain; to strive to understand the confusing and often irrational thoughts that abound."

However, his book is not aimed only at psychological transformation. It also traces Titus' inner journey of working through his anguish and, like Job in the Old Testament, confronting the great spiritual question that arises whenever disaster strikes: what sort of God allows suffering to happen to innocent people and how does one respond?

"I don't believe for a second that God mapped out a grand plan that included the murder of my daughter. By the grace of God, we are given free will, and in that free will, evil (in other words, self-love) is allowed to manifest alongside divine love and wisdom. But through the temptations presented by evil, love and truth will ultimately prevail, because that is God's will for us."

I had the opportunity to hear John Titus speak in 2004 and I met with him and Bev in spring 2011 as he was preparing the final drafts of this book. They are authentic people with deep souls and caring hearts. They know how to love and how to express it.

Americans can learn from Titus, especially since most of us have shut off our feelings about 9/11 long ago and allowed ourselves and our country to react impulsively and violently against the perpetrators.

John Titus did not write this book expecting or wanting sympathy or pity for the loss of Alicia. Instead, his words evoke love and compassion in the reader's heart which, he exclaims, is what life is all about.

Then again, readers will see how Alicia's murder prompted Titus to action. He pours over all the materials he can find on 9/11 and, through legal action, he insists on government accountability regarding its knowledge of terrorist activities and plans. Here we see a responsible father deeply motivated to protect his family.

He is also an empathetic man who literally reaches out to families in Afghanistan whose fallen loved ones have inadvertently gotten themselves in the way of American retaliatory justice.

He has been a spokesman for Peaceful Tomorrows (http://peaceful-tomorrows.org), an organization comprised of 9/11 families who have turned their grief into action for peace; held forums on peace at his place of employment, Schoolcraft College (Detroit); and set up a peace foundation at his alma mater, Urbana University (Ohio).

He even ran the San Francisco marathon, something Alicia had planned to do, because he believed the discipline of training could help his own healing and honor his daughter.

Titus did all of these things with Bev's love, support and participation. Instead of drifting apart, which happens in so many marriages after the death of a child, their relationship with each other and with their entire family grew stronger. He also did it through the spiritual presence and encouragement of Alicia, whom he believes was the essence of love and compassion.

Clearly, Titus and his family, are God's chosen ones called to address the unsavory violence lodged against innocent civilians, so characteristic of our current era. They are there for the rest of us to witness and emulate. This is a tremendous burden for one family but they have willingly taken it on even though they never sought it.

Titus provides a vivid, honest and often poetic presentation that is so compelling readers will not be able to put it down before they finish it. Ideally, people will read the book with family, friends and neighbors in order to reflect on 9/11 from a new perspective—and to help influence this nation's movement away from endless war and retaliation. What we need most, now, is peace within ourselves and among others in the world and John Titus shows us how to do it.

Olga Bonfiglio is a freelance writer and author of *Heroes of a Different Stripe*

Acknowledgements

First and foremost, I especially want to acknowledge and express my deep appreciation and undying love to my wife Bev; my children Alicia, Shanoa (Jay), Zachery (Lana), and Elijah; and my wonderful grandchildren Logan, Alexis, Isabella, and Alyson for enriching my life. Life would be so much less without you. And to my dear friends, co-workers, and extended family: for being there when I needed you, I thank you.

Throughout my journey of grief and healing I have been surrounded by loving, wise, and compassionate people. I hold in my heart my spiritual family from many religious and spiritual backgrounds—in particular the ministers and friends from the Swedenborgian Church of North America, who have been with me every step of the way with loving guidance and deep understanding; and Marianne Williamson, who personally inspires me and is such a powerful force for peace.

This book is dedicated to all who have lost loved ones to political violence. I am truly blessed to have met and been inspired by peacemakers from all over the world. I give special thanks to "my best friends I never wanted to know," September 11th Families for Peaceful Tomorrows, for truly understanding my grief and for your undying courage in the face of much adversity, sadness, and pain. To all the incredible people who are working diligently to make this world better through your tireless efforts to bring about peace and justice, my heart is forever with you.

A special thanks to Leah Goodwin for her expert editing, Shanoa for helping me to the finish line, Mike Major for the amazing cover artwork, and Sabrina and the wonderful people at Friesen Press.

Last, but certainly not least, I am so blessed and feel especially grateful to my daughter Alicia for bringing light and love into my life and the lives of so many others during her twenty-eight years and three months on this earth. You still inspire me!

About the Cover

The painting was done in my small studio at the Ansonia Hotel in 1973. It was a breakthrough kind of painting after many frustrating months of not doing creative work. The painting emerged out of risk-taking. Reaching for something "new" and unsafe was the motivation. The result was perhaps the most spiritual painting I have ever done and I kept going back to it as John and I discussed the qualities of Alicia.

Michael Major is a professional visual artist with over 35 years of experience and was the first artist-in-residence for the state of Ohio. Currently, he is creating a monument out of a section of steel from the WTC's South Tower to be dedicated on the tenth anniversary in Urbana, Ohio to Alicia and all who died on September 11, 2001.

As I entered the studio I was drawn repeatedly to the painting on the back wall. It reminded me of the "vision" I had of Alicia's soul rising from the rubble of the World Trade Center while helping the other souls find their way out of the mire and confusion. To me, it inspires hope in the midst of hopelessness and despair. When Mike suggested it for the cover, I was deeply moved and appreciative. Ironically, he painted this in New York City the summer Alicia was born.

John Titus

Losing Alicia

A Father's Journey After 9/11

Alicia Nicole Titus, 2000

Introduction

Throughout my life I've embraced the inevitable changes that come with spiritual growth and development. After all, we are spiritual beings living in human form, and change is an intricate part of that process. Even the difficult and painful transformations that result from loss can lead to new growth and soul regeneration.

But change doesn't come easily. The anguish-ridden process of grieving a loved one's death forces us to scrutinize our own life journey. Not only do we feel immense emptiness from the absence of our loved one, but we also remember our own mortality, our shortcomings, our failures, and our lost hopes and dreams. Even more profoundly, grief forces us to experience feelings that seem too tender, too raw, and far too painful. No one wants to feel so exposed and utterly helpless, whatever the potential for spiritual growth.

My family and I didn't have a choice in the matter. On September 11, 2001, my beloved daughter, Alicia, died violently, murdered by terrorists. All she had done to put herself in harm's way was go to work and reach out with kindness to those who were hell-bent on killing her and the many others who would die on that day.

That day, which had started out so gloriously sunny, soon became the darkest day of my life. My sweet, loving daughter's physical existence was savagely obliterated. As a family, we had to face our most horrific nightmare imaginable—and it only grew worse. Alicia's murder exposed the worst of human behavior, the evil of twisted religiosity, the ugliness of politics, and the blatant social injustices rampant in our world.

And this journey of grief did not take place in a vacuum. The media was in a feeding frenzy and our government was determined to go to war in retaliation: in short, the vicious cycle of violence was certain to continue. Our grief was publically exposed, scrutinized, politicized, analyzed, and internationalized. We became a 9/11 family.

Chapter 1

Loss and Grief, Politics and Religion

Needless to say, the violent murder of your child is not something you just "get over." Grief work is labor-intensive, life-changing, and excruciating—a highly emotional and spiritual process that doesn't just unfold in nice, clear-cut stages as studies may suggest. I'm a trained counselor with a master's degree in mental health counseling who holds two licenses that say I'm qualified to help others with mental health issues. But I was not prepared for the onslaught of feelings, nor the pervasiveness and intensity of the grief, that came with such a horrific loss. I found myself longing for this madness to end, but the sad reality is that there is no escape. During the first weeks and months I felt an overwhelming urge to run away, to escape somehow from the searing pain and intense trauma that had suddenly consumed my life. But when the shock faded, I realized that I had to face the music: the only way to deal with this all-consuming grief was to travel through its very heart. Some may delay the grieving process but eventually we must learn to cope—and it's an agonizing journey.

I knew that grief work would take some time. It's said that in "normal" grief it takes three to five years before full acceptance of a loss is recognized, but the complications surrounding the politicized, high-profile murder of your child make that process far lengthier. Not only do you have to confront grievous loss, but you are also faced with various legal issues and pending lawsuits, not to mention questions of culpability, underlying causes, societal impact, spiritual reckoning, political fallout, media depictions and coverage...and the list goes on. Though early on I tried to avoid the media frenzy about her murder, I was constantly exposed to it in some form or another: splashed across the front pages of magazines at the grocery checkout counter, in news flashes that popped up as I passed a TV, in radio news blurbs that interrupted normal programming, on talk shows, in conversations among complete strangers while sitting on a train, in our government's military response, in the terrorist alert systems implemented at airports—and, most of all, in the way that people treated us differently or avoided us entirely. My family and I had no time to grieve quietly. There was no privacy, no peace, except for a few stolen moments during which we retreated from the world and sought the solace of Mother Nature. I have witnessed my daughter's murder hundreds of times: it happens each time I watch the fiery explosion of the Boeing 767 crashing into the South Tower of the World Trade Center. I cannot escape this ghastly sight, which is permanently inscribed on my mind and heart.

Outwardly, each time I witnessed this tragic event, I became more and more numb to it. Inwardly, the sight set off a series of responses, a never-ending chain reaction of emotions in the deepest recesses of my soul. I tried to describe how this affected me in the journal that I kept during the first year after Alicia's death, but the experience is virtually indescribable. There is no way to begin to understand how such an experience affects you without experiencing it firsthand. I wouldn't wish such a nightmare on my worst enemy. At times I felt as if I myself were dying. In my journal, I described the feeling as the sensation of spiraling downward into a deep, dark abyss, wondering if I would ever find my way back out. At times I didn't care whether I did or not. I wanted to die too. If it weren't for my family's love and my faith in a loving God, life would have been unbearable.

Keeping a journal during this difficult time in my life served as means to process mentally, as an outlet for the barrage of emotions that were utterly confusing and completely overwhelming, and as a way of gauging my progress (or regress). Whenever I would write or reread what I had written, I would cry painful, ugly, beautiful, healing tears until there were none left. Weeping like this was hard for me, for I had been taught that "men don't cry." But if you don't allow yourself to cry, the healing will take longer. Studies have shown that tears of grief contain chemical toxins. If you don't allow these to release through the normal process of crying, they stay in your system and will manifest in some form or another. I can't imagine the destructive power of the pent-up anger and rage that would have plagued me had I not allowed myself to cry.

Journaling, for me, was very cathartic. I highly recommend it as an outlet for dealing with life's issues, especially those that are intensive and life-changing. Journaling became my time to grieve, communicate with Alicia, and commune with God. Journaling helped me to heal.

There is no road map for grieving, though it has been studied and written about in great detail. Our society is quite misinformed about the phenomenon. People often say (and did say to me), "Once you get back to work you'll feel better," or "Time heals," or "It will get better." All these assurances contained a germ of truth, but I wasn't ready to hear them—I needed time to grieve, and the grief was completely overwhelming. Another platitude I heard far too often was "God must have wanted her to come home," a claim that conjured up images of God plucking her from her vibrant life and placing her in harm's way; and "She's at peace now," which I knew to be true but found thoroughly unhelpful. The most absurd response I heard in response to the news of Alicia's death was "You're kidding me!" People don't know what to say or do when confronted with death; some just avoid the subject like the plague. Even some of my extended family members tried to act as if nothing had happened and attempted to create a sense of normalcy. Some would say, "I didn't want to bring it up because I was afraid to upset you"—as if I weren't already upset. But some loving souls were able to tune into our pain and, through a touch, a hug, a look, or a few heartfelt words of love, give us tremendous comfort. This is true empathy and genuine compassion. This is love in action.

The aftermath of Alicia's death was a confusing time. I felt as though all the cells of my body had been chaotically rearranged and my brain had gone permanently into overload. There really is no "right way" to deal with grief of this nature. It's a highly individualized process. But I'm not one to sit passively by and let life dictate my course of action, my state of wellbeing, or my spiritual journey. Even though I recognized the symptoms of depression and at times felt like succumbing to its powerful grip, I knew I had to overcome its debilitating force and trudge onward. At times I truly felt like I was merely "trudging"; it felt as though the weight of the world was on my shoulders. Through the grace of God; the love of my family, especially my wife, Bev; and special friends, I somehow found the strength to put one foot in front of the other and move forward. Sometimes it was two steps forward and one back, but it was progress, nonetheless.

Early in my grief journey, I spent a lot of time alone out in nature communing with God. It was the only place where I could find a sense of peace and serenity—life with people around seemed so painfully chaotic and nonsensical. Normal conversations about daily woes, TV shows, and sporting events seemed to pervade everyone's conversations. They all seemed absorbed in the mundane, but all the while I was screaming on the inside. For most people, life went back to normal soon after 9/11, even in the midst of a war in which innocent people like Alicia were dying every day. For us, though, the world was utterly screwed up. We felt the pain and suffering of the grieving parents whose sons and daughters were being killed by the weapons of our technically advanced war machine. And, through the grace of God, we had come to feel deep empathy and compassion for those Afghani and Iraqi parents whose children, our government, hell-bent on vengeance fueled by power and greed, was placing in harm's way. America's bellicose response to the 9/11 attacks would become a political agenda for President Bush's cabinet, taken directly from several of Bush's cabinet's document, the "Project for the New American Century."[1] Justice would take a backseat to the overriding desire to oust Saddam Hussein and create a strong military presence in the Middle East. America and the world would suffer as a result.

Some might think that losing a child at the hands of a radical group of religious fanatics would predispose us to an "eye for an eye" response, that we would want vengeance for the murder of our daughter. But it's much more complicated than that. Did we want justice for those responsible? Absolutely. But more killing of innocent people in our daughter's name? Absolutely not. Alicia was a "civilian casualty," her death the product of extremist jihadist thinking and a failed political system. Killing more blameless individuals in response would only exacerbate the problem and intensify hatred for America. This is exactly what bin Laden had planned and hoped for as a result of the 9/11 attack—he wanted to unify extremists in the Muslim world against us, the "infidels."

It soon became quite clear to Bev and me that answers to our questions about the murder of our daughter were not going to come easily. There was much more taking place behind the scenes—political maneuvering and the pursuit of hidden agendas of those in power, the leaders of our own government—that we weren't being told about. I soon found myself on a mission to understand all there was to know about the 9/11 attack and its underlying causes. I had to know. I could not turn a blind eye. I knew this attack on America had to be the product of much more than the politically crafted catchphrase "evil-doers who hate our freedom." This act of terrorism was indeed an evil act, but underlying factors had triggered this vicious attack. In the eyes of many, America, the world's economic and moral leader, had ignored the plight of our fellow human beings in economically deprived countries. We had desecrated Islam's Holy Land in Saudi Arabia with our cultural insensitivity and militaristic actions, especially during the first Gulf War while our troops were stationed there. And we had allowed the ongoing Israeli-Palestinian conflict, the epicenter of the Mideast conflict, to fester and deteriorate while providing billions of dollars for the Israeli military. In the irrational reasoning of bin Laden and others, America needed to be taught a lesson. This is the venomous hatred called evil. My daughter became a victim of all of this contorted, egotistical political nonsense.

I didn't set out to be a political activist. I just knew that what had happened to Alicia, not to mention the ensuing cycle of violence, had to stop. In my grief, it was hard for me to decide what clothes I would wear to the funeral service or whether I wanted to eat or what on earth to do next, but it soon became abundantly clear that I had to do all I could to stop this retributive killing and the civilian casualties that are so prevalent in war. References by our military and political leaders to these human deaths as "collateral damage" made me gasp. Did those who had killed her consider my daughter "collateral damage"? Had she been merely an expendable pawn in the larger game of war and politics? This dehumanizing of the enemy is intentional, but it will not help us find peaceful solutions nor learn to live in harmony with our neighbors.

And, by the way, I do see our Muslim friends as neighbors. I draw a clear distinction between moderate Muslims and extremists, just as I do between moderate and extremist Christians. Some Christians may find this idea appalling—how can I consider Muslims my equals when they don't believe in Christ? My question for them is this: How would Jesus feel about it? Didn't he say to love our enemies and care for our neighbors? Didn't he say "Blessed are the peacemakers"? Didn't he seek out those who were troubled, those who hungered, and those who had been cast aside? He didn't discriminate against those with backgrounds and beliefs different from his.

I'm a realist guided by a healthy dose of idealism. I don't live with my head in the clouds and think that, by some magic, all will be well and life will automatically be good. I can see evil and have been a victim of its hateful, destructive forces. But stooping to its level by doing more of the same, even vicariously through my government's actions, is not the way to combat evil. Our actions must be guided by God's love and wisdom. Despite our imperfections, we must strive to understand God's truth, not our own self-serving, ego-driven versions of it. We must also nurture our love in conjunction with truth and act in accordance with love and truth for the good of others. If we create more injustice by destroying entire cities and villages, along with thousands of innocent lives, in the midst of proclaiming our own self-righteousness, we lose touch with the divine principles of love and wisdom. Ultimately, we lose touch with God.

Some may wonder how I can talk about peace, justice, and America's shortcomings when our country has been attacked. I have been threatened on several occasions by people who disagreed with my views. Some have told me that my daughter deserved to die because of my views on human compassion, peace, and justice. But herein lies my dilemma: I'm not an uncompromising pacifist. I greatly admire those who are willing to give their lives to change the world in non-violent ways—people like Gandhi, Martin Luther King, Jr., and, of course, Jesus. They demonstrated incredible courage in the face of hatred and aggression and advocated strongly for change in response to injustice. I believe very strongly that those responsible for the murder of my daughter and nearly three thousand others on that day should be brought to justice. But what does that justice look like? Do we wage all-out war, ensuring the destruction of everyone and everything surrounding the perpetrators and devastating two countries in the process? Do we create another "crusade" against the terrorists, as President Bush so clumsily put it? Or could America have collaborated with the world community after the September 11 attack, engaged in a concerted effort with those countries that expressed empathetic allegiance to us at the time, and through our collaborative efforts, brought those responsible for this heinous crime to justice in an international court of law? This is what many of the victims' families suggested immediately after our loved ones were murdered. Would it have been easy? Absolutely not. But the approach America ultimately took has not worked. Millions of innocent people have died or been driven from their homes, we have lost thousands of young Americans in the process and spent billions and billions of dollars that could have been used for the greater good, and we still have not found a peaceful resolution. Al Qaeda and other terrorist organizations are still waging jihad against the "infidels" and killing innocent people—and they have garnered more support than ever. Our actions have, in effect, established another generation of committed terrorists. Many in the United States will justify our "War on Terror" by hiding behind the illusion that we have not been attacked since 9/11. But in reality, more terrorist activities are occurring around the world now than ever before. Declaring war has not solved the problem of terrorism, nor has it addressed the underlying issues that led to the 9/11 attacks. Violence only leads to more violence.

These realizations and much more have been a part of my grieving process. The journey has been complicated, painful, exasperating, troublesome, and extremely difficult. It has been long and promises to be longer. Like I said, I'm not one to sit on my hands and passively watch the world go by. I refuse to succumb to victim status. At times, I have had to let go of the politics behind my daughter's death, for sanity's sake. But as a citizen in this democracy I have an obligation to hold my elected officials accountable. I was totally at odds with the direction the Bush administration took in response to 9/11, and I can certainly find fault with the current administration's tactics. I do believe, however, that the Obama White House sees the issue from a loftier perspective. I say this knowing that some who read this assertion will throw the book down in disgust.

Fear is a powerful force. I remember thinking when my daughter was born that if anyone ever tried to do her harm I would be willing to kill, sacrifice my own life, or do whatever it took to stop it. When she was murdered, all I could feel was deep sadness and excruciating pain. I didn't feel hatred or vengeance. I couldn't see how that would aid my grieving, bring about any sense of justice or closure (an overused concept, in my opinion), or in any way improve the situation. As a matter of fact, had I allowed myself to sink into that pit of despair, of vengeance, anger, and hatred, my grief would have intensified and my soul hardened. Instead, I can honestly say that I have developed a greater compassion, deeper love, and renewed joy that would not have been possible had I let the venom of hatred consume me.

For many people struggling to survive in this world, justice is unfathomable and peace is a faraway concept with little meaning. For the three billion people who live on less than two dollars per day, or those grieving families who watch their children (over thirty thousand of them a day) die due to lack of food or medicine, or those who have been victimized by corrupt governments and systematic genocide, or those who live with war every day, or those without any hope of a better life, life must seem awfully cruel. Even in the United States of America, millions live in poverty, and many have no hope for a brighter tomorrow. Violence is a daily threat. The American Dream has long ago been shattered or never existed for these individuals at all. I know—I worked with youth facing these circumstances early in my career.

Many people respond that they are not their brothers' keepers. I say we do have a shared responsibility for other beings and all of life. If we don't care for our fellow human beings, then we can't possibly care for God. If we don't work toward peace and justice for all, how can we hope for these things for ourselves? If we stand idly by while those around us are suffering, how can we develop compassion and love in a world that too often seems devoid of both? Do you live by the Golden Rule—"do unto others as you would have done to you"? Or do you abide by the maxim "it's a dog-eat-dog world"? Or perhaps you even believe, as some claim, that "might makes right." The question that comes to mind is this: are you guided by your own self-serving ego, or does a higher power guide you? Does the world revolve around you, or do you see yourself in relation to the whole? These are tough questions, and if we answer honestly, we may not like what we see. But through the grace of God and our own willingness, we can change.

My own grief work brought all of these questions to light. I felt as though my soul had been laid open—my heart felt the pain of all those who have suffered. I received clarity in response to my humility and openness to truth, which was unfiltered by my shattered ego. Perhaps this is the gift that comes from such a tragedy, the blessing that comes from loss and suffering. Perhaps this is the grace of God willing us onward to become closer to a world of love for each other and a greater understanding of truth.

After his daughter was murdered on September 11 aboard United Airlines Flight 93, Derrill Bodley and other members of the 9/11 families visited Afghanistan and witnessed firsthand the destruction and devastation caused by our weapons of war. He met with survivors who had lost entire families, homes, and villages to our weapons. His compassion for them was personal and heartfelt. In a statement to the media, he noted that he had no more moral authority than anyone else, then went on to say that we all have this capacity for compassion within us—it's just that some of us have not awakened to ours yet.[2]

His heartfelt words convey the untold power of grief and loss better than most. Our suffering is not a punishment from God, as some might believe. Through our suffering, we are given opportunities to grow our souls, expand our understanding, and become more compassionate human beings. On the other hand, we can become bitter, hateful, and isolated from those around us. Both are compelling forces. I knew that I still had choices in responding to this maddening grief. Even though life had become oppressive and I felt incredible pain, sadness, and desolation, I knew that my free will remained intact. I knew that the grace of God was still present within me. I knew what I had to do for the sake of my own soul.

Thus began the journey—a journey I had to make. Each morning I would awaken early to meditate, pray, read, write, cry, and go out into nature to regenerate. This routine may sound all well and good, but life seemed deeply cruel. I yearned to feel a sense of peace and love in my soul, for all around swirled the forces of death, destruction, and hatred.

People were jumping on the "war wagon" at an alarming rate. Every day we were inundated with images of "weapons of mass destruction" in Iraq that didn't exist, visions of the "white cloud" of atomic destruction that wasn't real, the mutilation of young soldiers by chemical and biological weapons, a fictional image. All of this propaganda was conjured up to elicit fear and therefore support for a political agenda driven by short-sighted, self-serving politicians. All of it was sold to the world as a justifiable response to the killing of my daughter Alicia and all the others on 9/11 by al Qaeda terrorists who had no connection with Saddam Hussein. The war in Afghanistan, not to mention the shock-and-awe campaign, were half-baked, ill-conceived attempts to bring those responsible to justice, but it soon became evident that the strategy was just a stepping stone to another war with an agenda dominated by revenge, power, greed and politics.

At times, when I wrote in my journal (italicized sections), inspiration seemed to shine through. I would read something I had written and think that, for once, it truly conveyed what I was trying to express. I was reading extensively about grief, politics, and religious beliefs to gain deeper understanding and greater insight. What I read about grief always seemed so inadequate and predictable in its description of neatly defined stages. No books mentioned the relentless torment, the endless tears that can come at any moment, the sense of utter hopelessness, or the depth of the despair. I could feel the ache in my soul; the feeling of loss and desolation was overwhelming. Living became an intolerable chore.

Because of the twisted nature of Alicia's murder, innocence and trust were no longer a given for me. If it hadn't been for my grandson, with his pure heart and the deep, abiding love he gives so freely with such innocence and grace, I would have struggled even more. He was just a year and a half old when Aunt "Lish" was killed, but he remembers her; his soul remembers her. Alicia was there at his birth and whenever he was sick or his mom, my daughter Shanoa, needed help. Alicia joked to everyone that Logan was her baby and that Shanoa was just caring for him in her absence. It was a joyous sight to see her loving, maternal side come to life. She told her mom that when she held Logan in her arms "it made [her] ovaries scream." We were excited to witness the blossoming of her maternal instincts. She would have been a wonderful mom.

When I visited Logan during his little-boy years, after Alicia's death, he would grab my hand and say, "C'mon, Papa, let's go play." We would retreat to his bedroom and play at some creative adventure that he would conjure up. When that faraway, sad look drifted into my eyes, Logan would gently hold my face with his hands, look me in the eyes, and say, "No, Papa, let's play." He made me stay in the "here and now" and view the world from his perspective.

When he was three he asked me, "Papa, are we best friends?"

I responded, "We sure are."

"Will we be best friends forever, Papa?"

"We certainly will be," I said enthusiastically.

"I'll love you forever, Papa," he said, with complete conviction and purity of heart.

At that moment it was as if God had zapped me with a huge dose of pure love; my weary heart leaped for joy. He was and is truly a godsend.

Family and true friends are vitally important in our lives, especially during times of sorrow. I was raised to understand the importance of extended family. Aunts, uncles, cousins, and grandparents were a big part of my life; we gathered often during the year for family reunions. I even lived with my grandparents for a while when I was fourteen, when Grandpa was ill and needed help on the farm. As a family, we laughed and played together— and we also mourned together. So, during this most difficult time in my life, I needed family. Had I been all alone in trying to deal with this convoluted grief and intense sadness, I would have crawled into a hole and given up. Or perhaps I would have become a bitter alcoholic, a stoner, or a crotchety old man.

Actually, I can't imagine going through my grief alone or allowing myself to give up, though at times it did feel like an unbearable burden. Thankfully, I felt God's presence very profoundly, even in the depths of my grief, but family and friends helped manifest His goodness through their compassion and love.

We all grieve in different ways and at our own pace. When in relationship with others, this uniqueness complicates the process significantly. Bev was grief-stricken, depressed, and distraught; she couldn't sleep and was deeply saddened. A mother's bond to her child is so strong! Alicia was Bev's firstborn and became her best friend and mentor. They had a very special relationship, a deep and lasting bond. Then our daughter was gone, torn from us by hate-filled terrorists who knew nothing about her. Even today the immense pain and sadness is very real and manifests unpredictably. Our remaining children struggled with the murder of their big sister, even though they tried to keep their feelings in check around us. There were periods of anger, deep-seated anger that would rear its ugly head and overpower any sense of reason. But anger is a part of grief and must be dealt with in a non-destructive way—otherwise the anger becomes a volcano inside us and erupts without notice. It hurt my soul to see my family suffer. Bev and I struggled together, but there were times when the pain of the other, compounded with our own pain, was more than either of us could take. Yet through it all we found an even greater love for each other.

Grief has a baffling regenerative power. Though it can destroy, it can also deepen compassion, intensify love, and grow understanding. Even when it seemed that I had no recourse, that my fate had been sealed, I realized I still had free will. I could still choose the path ahead of me. Perhaps I'll look back someday at my chosen path with the conviction that it really has "made all the difference," as Robert Frost so eloquently put it. For now, it truly does feel like "the road less travelled by,"[1] but I shall see it through to my journey's end.

---

[1]   Robert Frost, "The Road Not Taken," from the collection *Mountain Interval*, 1916.

Alicia with a glass of wine

Ten-year-old Alicia on a Tyrolian Traverse

Alicia, Greg and Logan, 2001

Alicia, Dad and Logan, 2000

Alicia's family, August 2000

Chapter 2

The Day That Forever Changed My Life

Life is fraught with changes, even though we strive to find a sense of constancy and minimize the unpredictability. You just never know what is going to happen next. After years of struggling to make ends meet, raising children, earning college degrees, and working diligently to provide for the basics, I always retained the hope that life would get better along the way. Then, when at last we were getting to the point where all the hard work, soul searching, growing pains, hopes, and prayers were giving back and life was in balance, tragedy struck. My world was devastated, my hopes and dreams were shattered and my worst nightmare had just become a reality. "Dear God," I thought, "from whence comes the strength to go on?"

"Time heals all wounds," they would say with such conviction. I heard this and other preprogrammed responses over and over again in those early days after Alicia's murder as caring people tried to comfort us in our grief. In my heart I knew the ugly truth: it would never get better. Alicia was dead. My heart was shattered. People assume that time does heal all wounds. At this stage in my grieving the sadness and pain seem endless; I honestly don't see how time will heal this wound. This wound is deeply spiritual and painfully emotional; it may never heal. It penetrates the soul and has left a gaping wound not unlike the ghastly hole left in the South Tower of the World Trade Center when my daughter's plane exploded into it at 500 miles per hour. I have accepted that the healing may take a lifetime or more. Time does bring with it a sense of reprieve, and I am learning to cope with the intense pain, but the sadness will always be a part of me. The violent murder of my beloved Alicia, my firstborn child, has left a void in my life that will forever haunt me. My soul cries out for relief. My heart yearns for healing love and my mind searches for understanding. Help me, God!

It has been over three years since that tragic day that forever changed my life. I often think back to that horrific day and feel the intense pain as if it were only yesterday. I am resigned to the fact that immense yearning and deep sorrow will always dwell within me. I know my wounded heart will always remain unhealed at some level. I must learn to live with this endless ache and the deep sadness that threatens my wellbeing. I also know I must learn to cope with the heartache and not let it destroy me, for the temptation to succumb is a powerful force. Somehow, I will find a new way to experience joy once again. I will continue to grow spiritually. I will persist in my search for greater love and wisdom to guide me along life's journey. One thing I know for certain: I feel passionately resolute in my conviction to dedicate my life to making this devastated world better—in spite of the pain, in spite of the disillusionment, in spite of the twisted terrorists who killed my daughter. This is my newly defined purpose in life, which has emerged like the phoenix rising from the ashes of the fiery ruins at Ground Zero in New York City. (Journal, November 2004)

*   *   *

On that dreadful September morning in 2001, I distinctly remember thinking how utterly magnificent the cloudless blue sky was as I made my way eastward down the tree-lined country road on my way to work. On days such as this I often say a silent prayer in appreciation for such radiance and glory. It comes from Psalm 118: "This is the day the Lord hath made; let us rejoice and be glad in it." I completed the forty-five minute drive to work and felt invigorated by the splendor of the morning. How quickly it all changed!

After settling in at my office and grabbing my notebook, I headed to the staff meeting room. I was leading the discussion when, all of a sudden, my co-worker Gail burst through the door, hurried toward the television, and turned it on. She was saying something about an airplane crashing into the World Trade Center. The news reporter was speculating about it being an accident and how such a thing could possibly happen.

I knew immediately that this was no accident. I watched in horror as smoke and flames spewed from the North Tower, just as another plane came into view. I noticed the time; it was 9:03 a.m. The second plane banked at an extreme angle as it circled toward the building and crashed into the South Tower in a fiery explosion. I learned later that it was United Airlines Flight 175 flying out of Boston and destined for Los Angeles.

My first thought was, "Oh, my God. What on earth is going on?" Immediately, I felt a surge of confusion, then an immediate sense of compassion and overwhelming sorrow for those who had been killed or injured and for their loved ones left behind. I also wondered what on earth would motivate someone to destroy the lives of hundreds of innocent people. What had our world come to? It was truly a sad day in the history of mankind, a clear statement that something was terribly amiss in our world. The misery others in the world felt had hit home: now America would be made to feel the horror of war, death, and destruction on her shores. The aftereffects would linger for years to come.

We cut our staff meeting short and talked for a few minutes about the horrendous tragedy we had just witnessed. A coworker mentioned that the planes were thought to be from American Airlines, but there was some speculation that one of them was a United Airlines plane. I felt a jolt of fear surge through my body with this unthinkable possibility, but denial would serve to protect me for a little while longer.

Meanwhile, at our home near Dexter, Michigan, my wife, Bev, had been starkly awakened around 8:42 a.m. She'd had a late night and was trying to catch up on her sleep; she tried to shake it off, but thought she heard a woman's voice calling to her. I remember her saying that it sounded like Alicia, our oldest daughter, crying out for help. But that couldn't be; she was in Boston or on a plane somewhere doing her job as a flight attendant for United Airlines. We knew that because she had tried to take off work to come be with us. Our grandson, Logan, had been staying with us for a few days, and we had needed someone to watch him that Tuesday morning while Bev and I worked. Alicia had hoped to be there to help out, but she couldn't take the day off. She had only worked for the airline for nine months and didn't yet have enough seniority.

Alicia loved travel and cherished meeting people from all over the world. Her previous employment in the corporate world hadn't allowed her the time or freedom to do so. Working as a flight attendant gave her the freedom to do it all: she could travel, had autonomy and flexibility, and finally had the time to go back to school for her postgraduate degree in teaching. She loved learning and teaching others how to enjoy life. She was an intelligent, warm-hearted "people person" who thoroughly enjoyed helping others and making the world a better place.

We found out later that at 8:42 a.m. the very moment at which Bev was pulled from sleep, the hijackers took over United Airlines Flight 175 in a violent, bloody coup. As if guided by some inner sense, she went directly to the television upon waking (something she never had done before), turned it on, and watched in horror as United Airlines Flight 175 crashed into the South Tower of the World Trade Center. Bev is an incredibly intuitive person and was immediately overcome with a sinking feeling of hopelessness and despair. She tried to shake it off as she prepared herself for work, but she knew at some level that something terrible had happened. I headed back to my desk feeling shaken and deeply introspective. I passed our receptionist, Gerry, and recall her asking me if I felt that this tragedy might be the result of karma. I answered that it must be some kind of perverse retribution against America, because the act was so violent and reprehensible and had specifically targeted innocent people. Surely the poor souls who were caught up in this did not deserve such hate and vengeance.

I went into my office, but my mind was not focusing on work. Something was amiss deep within my soul. I felt a profound angst and a growing sense of fear, both uncommon feelings for me. I was startled back into the here and now by the urgent ringing of the telephone on my private line. My youngest sister, Jodi, was on the other end.

"Johnny," she asked, "have you heard from Lish?"

No, I had not, but I could hear the worry in her voice, so I assured her that Alicia was fine. The words echoed back to me with the eeriness of a nightmare. *What are the odds?* I reasoned to myself. *I mean, there are thousands of flights going out every hour. Surely Alicia wasn't on one of those planes that crashed in New York City.* Jodi urged me to give United Airlines a call. She was going to call Alicia's roommates in Boston, where she had a secondary apartment at which she stayed when working.

I attempted to call United Airlines, but they weren't releasing any information yet. They assured me that when they had confirmed which flights were involved and who was aboard those flights, they would notify the families immediately. In the meantime, we could only wait in agony and fervently hope and pray for the best.

Jodi called back, her voice urgent, but she tried to maintain control. She said that Haley, a fellow flight attendant and roommate, had confirmed that Alicia was on United Airlines Flight 175. The problem was that UAL 175 had not been confirmed as the flight that had crashed. It was all speculation at this point, but the seeds of hopelessness were starting to germinate and the cloud of darkness was hovering. The deepest, darkest fears possible for a parent to have were taking form and starting to surface— fears so loathsome that merely to entertain them would surely inflict permanent damage on the psyche and unsettle the soul. The possibility that harm or death could come to one of my beloved children was unfathomable. Anything else in life I could handle, with God's help and the love of family and friends, but not the murder of my child. Dear God, no!

Although I knew rationally that what was done was done, nonetheless, I prayed desperately for Alicia's safe return—that somehow she had escaped this horrendous tragedy. The comforting veil of denial thus allowed me slowly to reconcile the stark reality that longed to destroy me. I was in the midst of chaos, the eye of a hurricane, and destruction swirled around me. As the endless minutes slowly ticked away and no word came from United, I felt my world starting to shatter. My heart pounded relentlessly, shifting into a "fight or flight" survival mode.

My love for my children is greater than I ever thought possible. I have always been a spiritual seeker; prior to having children, I struggled along on life's journey searching for meaning and purpose. But the first time I held my newborn daughter, I felt the divine within me come to life. I felt connected with all of existence through my child and knew at that moment that life would never be the same. God had granted me a miracle in the form of Alicia. When she was born, I knew I needed to rise to the occasion. I had to let go of my own ego-directedness, grow my understanding of truth, allow God's love to manifest through me more fully, and get on with making this world a better place, for my daughter's sake. June 11, 1973 was the first day of my new journey, and Alicia, in all of her radiant glory, was my inspiration and hope. All of the suffering in the world, all the ugliness that lurked in the shadows, all the hopelessness that destroys so many lives in every part of the world, seemed powerless in the face of such purity, such innocence, such joy and love.

This beautiful beginning contrasted starkly, ironically, with such a tragic, violent ending. My mind swirled and my heart throbbed. My hope was fading like a dying star in the waning night. How could I go on? How would I survive such a tragedy? God, help me!

Bev called. I could hear undertones of fear and pain in her voice. She had talked with Greg, Alicia's boyfriend who lived in San Francisco. He had heard that Alicia's flight was over Indiana, and we tried to digest this new information. It briefly gave us renewed hope.

Bev had also talked with our other daughter, Shanoa, who has always worn her emotions on her shirt sleeve. She had witnessed the airplane strike the South Tower also, and was nearly inconsolable with the fear that her big sister might be aboard. She loved Alicia dearly, and Alicia had always been a genuinely loving elder sister to her. Shanoa aspired to be more like Alicia, but her strengths were different, as was her beautiful personality.

Bev called Montana to wish our son Zac a happy birthday. He had been born on September 11, 1978. September 11 was also my paternal grandfather's birthday. Because of the time difference, Zac had neither seen nor heard about what was going on in New York City, Washington, D.C., and Pennsylvania. Bev wanted him to be aware of what was happening and assure him we would keep him informed. By a strange twist of fate, he would soon be the one who conveyed the tragic news to us. But that wouldn't happen for a couple more hours. In the meantime, the walls were closing in around us.

By now, we were hearing all kinds of distressing rumors and remnants of best-guess news reporting. Neither of us could concentrate on our work, so I invited Bev to come to my office until we heard something more reliable. I knew we had to be together, whatever the outcome.

Neither of us could face the possibility of receiving such a shock alone. We needed each other more than ever.

She arrived at my office at around 11:00 a.m. After a few more attempts to call United Airlines for some answers and some further telephone conversations with family, we decided to go home at around noon. I remember the looks of concern in my coworkers' eyes as we departed. I could feel their compassion and empathy.

The forty-five minute drive down North Territorial Road was very surreal and far too long. I barely noticed the bright blue sky on this beautiful autumn day. Earlier, I had been energized by the glorious weather. Now I was oblivious. My mind was a million miles away, and my soul was already crying out in pain.

As we opened the door to our two-story farmhouse sited next to the Huron River, the phone was ringing. I don't even remember who picked it up. At the other end was our son Zac. United Airlines had gotten his number from my mother-in-law. All I remember is feeling an overwhelming sense of panic and grief as he announced the dreaded news. We cried out with deep, agonized sobs. Our world had just exploded into a million pieces, just like the remains of my dear, sweet Alicia.

My eighteen-year-old son Eli was still at Dexter High School. I knew I had to go get him immediately. I called the principal and told him the terrible news; I was touched by his heartfelt response. Somehow I managed to drive the five miles to his school and walk through the front door. The principal escorted me into his office, gave me a hug, and sent for Eli. At my request, he left when Eli arrived. I told Eli what had happened as gently as I could, but my deep distress was painfully obvious. Eli burst into tears as we hugged each other in an embrace that encapsulated the utter desperation and powerful love we felt in that moment. On the way to the car, Eli's knees buckled from the weight of his grief and he nearly fell to the ground. We drove home in silence, but the screaming in my soul penetrated the air anyway, piercing the day's deceptive calm. My protective veil of disbelief had been replaced with an intense, unbearable pain that penetrated my whole being. My soul was in agony.

Chapter 3

The Journey Begins: An Inside Look at Grief

Despite all of my years of experience and education, both formal and informal, I had no point of reference to pull from for such a devastating and painful tragedy. Panic and reason wrestled for dominance. Misery seared my heart. An intimate part of my own being had just been destroyed. I searched my mind for answers, for some explanation, for guidance to help me on this journey I found myself taking. My prayers became desperate pleas for help. Thankfully, my mind numbed itself for fleeting moments, just long enough to deliver a thought. A part of me longed to lose myself in my misery and join my sweet Alicia on her journey in the great beyond. I wanted to find a way to help her through her transition, to hold her one more time, to protect her as only a father could. But it was too late. I could clearly see her standing before me in my mind's eye; her beautiful smile and angelic presence dazzled me, and she radiated a pure white light. It was definitely her. But I couldn't reach out and hold her.

Then another wave of grief hit me with the force of a giant ocean wave. This analogy felt very real, since a few months earlier I had tried to boogie board with my son off the north coast of Oahu, Hawaii. As I headed straight into a mountainous wave, it slammed me to the ocean floor, raking me across the sandy bottom and holding me down beneath the ocean's relentless, crushing force. I was sure I was going to drown. I struggled to the surface, gasped for air, and was hit by another wave of equal force. Somehow, miraculously, I managed to survive. Grief feels just like that, only the waves are inescapable and the pain is relentless. At times, I felt like I wanted to die. Sometimes I felt like running away. Sometimes I didn't feel at all. Always, my soul cried out in agony and despair, longing for cessation, for relief, for my daughter.

After sobbing uncontrollably until it felt as if no more tears were possible, Bev and I started calling loved ones and receiving calls. The word spread like wildfire. Friends and family offered up their deepest sympathies. I took tremendous comfort in knowing that so many people cared so much. It helped ease our burden, but only for a moment. The intensity of our grief grew as our bodies' protective shock mechanisms wore off. I felt desolate and cold. Bev, Eli, and I walked around like zombies, faraway looks in our eyes. Life had dealt us the worst blow imaginable. But somehow we would survive...or would we?

The events of the rest of that day are a blur of confusion, shock, and pain. Everything was surreal, a bad dream from which I couldn't awaken. Surely this was not real. Perhaps Alicia had missed her flight. Maybe somehow she had escaped death.

Later that day, our family started arriving from Ohio. The media hounds had also found us. Then an angel named Sandy appeared at our front door. She had been sent to offer us assistance and support and help us navigate these uncharted waters. United Airlines had heeded our unspoken call for help. Whether to salvage their public-relations image, maximize damage control, or express heartfelt concern, United Airlines had made arrangements for Sandy to walk with our family through the first days of mourning. She made sleeping arrangements for our arriving family members. She screened telephone calls and spoke with the media. She bought groceries and took care of the incoming food from care organizations. She tidied our house. She lent an empathic ear. She offered us loving hugs and a warm heart when the moment called for it. She helped us weather the storm, and didn't leave our side until after the memorial service was over. She was a godsend, and she will always hold a special place in my heart.

Chapter 4

A Prayer and a Vision

I grew up on a farm in mid-Ohio, immersed in the joys of nature and appreciating all of God's creation. As children, my brothers and I would spend endless days in the woods, hiking along streams, swimming in ponds and lakes, and playing games as though the entire wonderland had been put there just for our own enjoyment. Even our chores took place out in nature: we worked on the farm, taking care of animals, baling hay, cutting wood, and weeding the garden. I loved it. I felt deeply connected with God through nature. Consequently, when life felt oppressive or the burden would become too great to bear, I developed a habit of withdrawing into nature to find peace and rejuvenation. On the day Alicia died, I realized that I needed to retreat into nature. I needed to find someplace where this confusing life made sense once again.

Bev and I hiked up to Peach Mountain near our home, a place where I often go running, hiking, and mountain biking. I love running on the rugged trails, up and down the hills, through the pine forests, away from human influence. At times like these I am most connected with the Divine—I commune with God. Running often becomes meditation in motion for me as I catch the scents indigenous to the season, witness the deer running silently through the underbrush, see the squirrels scurrying about and chattering from a tree limb overhead, and listen to the symphonic sounds of the birds as they serenade me on my journey. I love it all. I love running in the freshly fallen snow, the bursting forth of new life in the spring, the hot summer days when the strong smell of the pine trees entices me, and, in the fall, running along the path of multicolored leaves with the pungent smell of decay in the air. On this day I barely noticed any of these things, though autumn was in its glory.

I ran along the path as hard as I could until I couldn't run anymore. The tears streamed down my cheeks and clouded my eyes. As I ran, I wept. I ran until I had returned to the overlook where we had started. This place provided an eagle's-nest view from which we could take in the valley below and gaze into the clear blue sky as the sun shone brightly in the western sky. Bev was there, looking deeply forlorn, covered in an all-consuming sadness and a haunting look of despair and pain. We embraced and sobbed together. We longed for release from this hell. We longed for our sweet Alicia to be with us. A prayer formed in my aching soul.

My dear, sweet Alicia,

My heart is broken. My soul cries out for reason. Everything seems so surreal. The sun is shining in all of its radiant glory; a gentle peace fills the woods; the deer saunter along in no apparent hurry; and God is all around. I know loved ones who have gone before and angels from on high are comforting you. But the pain I feel is so deep, so real…like a huge ocean wave, relentless with its crushing force; it pounds away at my heart.

There is so much of life I want to share with you. I long to feel your laughter in my soul; to see the joy in your eyes as you care for little Logan; to experience your exuberant spirit as it soars free as a bird; to experience your gentle love and the strength of your character…God, how I miss you. (Journal, September 11, 2001)

As Bev and I sat down on the precipice in solemn meditation, I prayed that God would come into our hearts. I prayed for understanding and love. I prayed for Alicia's soul and the souls of the others who had died with her earlier in the day. I prayed for our world.

As I was deep in meditation, I felt Alicia's presence and saw her in my mind's eye. She was radiant. Her smile was more magnanimous than ever. And she assured me that she was at peace and had transcended the chaos. She showed me the little child she had been holding in those last few moments before her death. I saw her holding him in the back of the airplane. His head was in her lap and she was soothing him, caressing his hair. A man sat on the other side of her, obviously the boy's father. The boy was about two or three years old, with blondish brown hair. He was comforted, and Alicia had a serene look on her face. In this moment before death, she had found the consoling presence of God, and I was reassured. She let me know that her soul was alive. But I still yearned to hold her in my arms.

Afterwards, we made our way back to the house, which by now was abuzz with family and friends who had come to comfort us and share in our grief. Some tried to act as if it were a normal family gathering, with talk about mundane things and occasional laughter; such moments were often followed by haunting silence and sudden tears. Grief is overpowering, and normalcy was not to be had. The pain was just too overwhelming. Grief is such a mysterious encounter, even in its predictability: one minute you're reminiscing and laughing; the next you're filled with a pain that could easily consume you with its destructive force. We would experience the gamut of emotions and encounter profound changes as we strove to regain our equilibrium and find once again our purpose for living.

Dreams are ambiguous, but they often give us insight into the complexities of life. They also can be premonitory. I recalled the dream I had had the night before this horrible day. In my dream, I was at a memorial service for someone who had died. I thought it was my own service. In retrospect, I realize that it was indeed an ominous glimpse of what was about to unfold. In my dream, hundreds of family and friends had gathered together to comfort one another and embrace the interconnectedness of our existence. Everyone I had ever known was there, reaching out to one another, giving support, caring, and loving. It all felt so real, so wonderfully divine with the sincerity of love and heartfelt compassion demonstrated. I wondered why, in real life, we tend to put off being so genuinely loving, so divinely human as God intended us to be with one another, until a death prompts us to do so. Why can't we do this more often in life when, in our hearts, we really do care for each other? What is it in human nature that allows us to settle for superficial interactions and a mundane existence void of true feelings and purity of thought? How do we become so disconnected from one another? When tragedy strikes, we see the true essence of life itself. We are given an opportunity to relate from our hearts, guided by truth itself, as God intends for us.

I mentioned before that I come from a large family. In my dad's family, there were eight boys and one girl, all of whom had children, who all had children, the numbers increasing exponentially with each generation. We gathered together for holidays, for celebrations, for homemade ice cream parties. My cousins were like siblings, and my aunts and uncles were like additional parents. We recognized family as existing beyond the confines of our individual households. This attitude helped me feel connected with generations gone by, helped me understand the interconnection of the human soul with God. I have four brothers and two sisters, all of whom have children and grandchildren. Our family is burgeoning; new additions arrive on a regular basis. Bev also comes from a large family, and everyone looks on her with great esteem. Faced with the daunting task of reconciling ourselves to our daughter's murder, we now found ourselves in dire need of love and comfort. We needed family and friends more than ever, and would for many days to come. Never before had we so desperately needed familial love.

The evening finally settled upon us. Minutes seemed like hours, hours like days. Nothing seemed real. I was exhausted, but my mind wouldn't shut off. If the day had produced such a horrendous night-mare, what did the night have in store? At some point I drifted off to sleep from sheer exhaustion, but I awoke sobbing. I didn't want to awaken Bev, but she hadn't slept at all. She immediately embraced me, soothed me, rocked me in her bosom, and so eased my pain. In the days, weeks, and years to come we would learn more completely the consoling power of love made manifest in each other's arms. We needed each other more than ever. The sad reality is that nearly eighty percent of the parents who lose a child end up divorced. I certainly can see why. Everything becomes a challenge. Normal, day-to-day tasks become major obstacles; mountains emerge from molehills; unresolved conflicts become pitched battles. It's hard to feel and give love when you're in such deep pain and in the throes of depression. But thank God for the healing power of marital love!

After Alicia's death, I read numerous books searching for answers, looking for ways of coping, longing for understanding. It helped, to a certain degree. One of the things that stood out in regard to relation-ships came from Rabbi Kushner's book *When Bad Things Happen to Good People*.[3] In his book, born from the death of his son, he talks about couples who lose children, and he uses the analogy of a team of horses pulling a heavy load. When the team works together, they manage to pull the weight, but only with great effort. When one falters, the other is left to pull the burdensome load along with the additional weight of the other. Resentment, anger, and blame are often the result. Each of us works through the phases of grief differently, and very often our processes are not in sync with each other. It's a tremendously heavy burden to carry; even when couples care deeply for each other and attempt to work together, the weight of the grief can be overwhelming.

Chapter 5

The Nightmare Continues

September 12 felt even more intense in some ways than the day before. Reality seeped through the protective veil of shock. It was ghastly. Thoughts of Alicia's last moments raced through my head: the overwhelming sense of helplessness in those last moments as the plane banked dramatically in its final 500-mile-per-hour swoop toward the largest building in the world; people screaming, vomiting, and being tossed around by the erratic piloting; panic filling the air with an impending sense of doom in those final seconds...and then the fiery crash.

Incessant thoughts. Painful thoughts. Sad thoughts. They played over and over in my head, and the visual replay was in my face everywhere I turned, on the front page of every newspaper and magazine, the major headline in every media blitz for days, weeks, months...forever, it seemed. Everywhere I turned, someone was talking about September 11. In my mind, September 11, the day of Alicia's murder, will always be foremost. I didn't need all of those graphic reminders and absurd commentaries. It all felt like salt in the wound. In the midst of that ball of fire, the headline-dominating image of the Boeing 767 crashing into the South Tower, the gruesome images of death and destruction, I could see Alicia's joyous smile and feel her comforting love. I knew that she was at peace and had taken her rightful place in the world beyond. The other vital message that came vividly through to me was that she would help us through this deluge of pain and confusion, this looming journey of grief that had been thrust upon us. She will always be with us, in our hearts, in our minds, and in our souls. She was there beside us in our hour of grief and always will be.

Most of our family was there with us as we wandered aimlessly around the house on that second day. Our son Zac and his wife, Lana, lived in Montana and couldn't fly in because all of the planes were grounded—the only exceptions being the planes authorized by the White House to take a Saudi contingent, which included thirty-two members of the bin Laden family[2], back to Saudi Arabia. Our country's leaders allowed these individuals to leave with little or no questioning by investigators, but that's another part of this whole ugly mess. Politics and religion, power and greed—we learn to tiptoe around all of these things in our daily lives so we don't upset one another and cause conflict. All of these things led to the killing of my innocent daughter and would surely haunt us forever.

Left with no other alternatives, Zac and Lana decided to rent a car and started on the daunting cross-country journey, carrying the burden of his sister's horrendous murder fresh in their minds as the miles rolled along. I can only imagine how grieved and helpless they must have felt as they drove along those desolate plains. We needed them home with us. We needed to grieve together and find strength and comfort with one another. We needed our remaining children and grandson where we could see them, hug them, and know that they were safe with us. Life seemed so perilous and untenable without them!

Out of Chaos, Clarity Emerges

As family and friends gathered at our home, Sandy made arrangements for their stay. Schoolcraft College, where I worked, brought trays of exquisitely prepared food from the Culinary Arts Program, which is one of the best in the world. Neighbors brought home-cooked food.

---

2   During his testimony at both the Senate Judiciary Committee and the 9/11 Commission hearings, Richard Clarke stated the following:

"Now, what I recall is that I asked for flight manifests of everyone on board and all of those names needed to be directly and individually vetted by the FBI before they were allowed to leave the country. And I also wanted the FBI to sign off even on the concept of Saudis being allowed to leave the country. And as I recall, all of that was done. It is true that members of the Bin Laden family were among those who left. We knew that at the time. I can't say much more in open session, but it was a conscious decision with complete review **at the highest levels of the State Department and the FBI and the White House**." Testimony of Richard Clarke, Former Counterterrorism Chief, National Security Council, before the Senate Judiciary Committee, September 3, 2003. (Emphasis mine.)

"I was making or coordinating a lot of decisions on 9/11 and the days immediately after. And I would love to be able to tell you who did it, who brought this proposal to me, but I don't know. Since you pressed me, the two possibilities that are most likely **are either the Department of State, or the White House Chief of Staff's Office**. But I don't know." Testimony of Richard A. Clarke before the National Commission on Terrorist Attacks Upon the United States, March 24, 2004. (Emphasis mine.)

Meanwhile, Sandy had already gone to the store and picked up enough food to feed an army. One thing was certain; we weren't going to go hungry. Friends wanted to help; the food kept appearing, along with flowers, cards, and telephone calls. The outpouring of warmth and love was consoling and much needed at a time when humanity had just dealt us a death blow and our faith in our fellow human beings had been so devastatingly shaken. We needed to feel goodness in the face of this evil; we needed love in its purest form; we needed hope when, all around, hopelessness prevailed; we needed to know that God had not forgotten us and that love and truth would overcome the hate, the violence, and the confusion.

I remember talking with newspaper reporters in those first few days. I vividly recall a redefined purpose emerging, in spite of the reality that my beloved daughter's life had just been violently snuffed out. *We must,* I thought, *stop the senseless killing of innocent people. When will this crazy cycle of violence end?*

From the beginning of recorded history, much of our human journey has revolved around finding more advanced means of destroying our fellow humans. And yet basic truths consistently appear in the writings of enlightened individuals, truths that have become the premise of most major religions. Chief among these is the uniting principle of "love thy neighbor." I often wonder: do religious leaders not believe this premise as a basic truth of their religion? Do otherwise religious people who claim to be following the path of God or Allah not understand the concept of "love" or of "neighbor"? Or does their definition limit the neighbor to those who are of like mind politically, ethnically, sexually, economically, and religiously? This unifying love for one another, professed by all major religions, became prominent in my thinking. I keep coming back to this idea because I think it is imperative to human survival that we all scrutinize it. From my perspective, the evolution of the human soul has lagged drastically behind our technological capabilities—our capability to develop weapons of mass destruction and use them against one another. We in the United States are just as guilty of this sin as others. After all, the terrorists who murdered my daughter used only knives, box cutters, and mace to accomplish their goal. We responded with weapons of mass destruction and missiles that epitomize the ultimate killing machine—billions of dollars' worth of the most advanced technology specifically designed to destroy our neighbor.

What if we utilized even a portion of that military money to eradicate disease in developing countries; or to feed, clothe, and house the three billion people who live in abject poverty; or to help stop the needless deaths of the thousands of children per day due to lack of medicine and food? What if we really did act on the teachings of Christ, Buddha, Mohammed, and others, and truly attempted to love our neighbors?

Instead, we find ways to divide and dehumanize, we resort fearfully to violence to resolve conflicts, we strike back with vengeance, and we sit in judgment of those different from us. And the killing of innocent people continues. God surely must have an abundance of patience, for it seems that we humans are indeed slow learners.

Chapter 6

From Whence Comes the Strength to Go On?

Zac and Lana finally arrived; Eli was home; and Shanoa, Jay, and Logan were with us, along with brothers, sisters, friends, parents, nieces, nephews—our family (minus our oldest daughter). There was laughter and frivolity; there were tears of pain and sorrow; there were moments of sharing bygone days; and there was an ominous sense of ever-present foreboding, a strange tension in the air that bespoke tragedy. We had the painful task of planning our beloved daughter's funeral ahead of us, a task no parent wants to think about.

Our loving friends and family took the lead, thank God, and guided us gently along as we started the process of making arrangements for Alicia's visitation and memorial service. We had no body to bury, not even a piece of her body. The only things of Alicia's they found were her driver's license and Boston Library card. They were slightly warped, but basically unscathed. The library card is emblematic of Alicia's love of reading. She was an avid reader, just like me, my siblings, my mother, my grandparents, and her sister. Alicia was on a constant quest for knowledge and always in search of life's fullest joys. Life experiences filled with adventure, travel, and reading were part of that quest. She read for pleasure, and she read for understanding in search of truth.

Bev and I have several good friends who are clergy, many of them in the Swedenborgian Church. Truths from the writings of Emmanuel Swedenborg[3] are, in my estimation, some of the best resources for

---

3 Swedenborg (1688-1772) shared in his theological writings a view of God as infinitely loving and existing at the very center of our beings, a view of life as a spiritual birthing as we participate in our own creation, and a view of Scripture as a story of inner life stages as we learn and grow. Swedenborg said, "All religion relates to life, and the life of religion is to do good." He also felt that the sincerest form of worship is a useful life.

the spiritual evolvement of the human soul. Swedenborgians, as the Christians who use his writings to interpret the Bible are called, don't proselytize as many Christian traditions do. They believe that each person has free will on his or her personal journey of regeneration, and that each person has a unique path toward divine love and wisdom that involves service to others, or "uses" in Swedenborg terminology.

I had grown up in a more conservative Protestant tradition and had studied other religions somewhat in college. As a young adult, I was open to many forms of true worship of God, the Great Mystery, as He is called in the Native American tradition. I have always been a spiritual person in search of greater understanding. Swedenborgian theology is incredibly deep and rich in its view of the human soul and the word of God, and prophetic in its vision for the development of the human soul. Swedenborg, with his exceptional analytical style of thinking and his divinely inspired, visionary view of the spiritual and celestial, expanded the realm of spirituality for me and opened new avenues for under-standing God's love and truth. Alicia's memorial service contained these elements and more. It was a concerted effort by many, spearheaded by our dear friends. Painful as it was, it was a spiritual experience in itself.

Chapter 7

Honoring Alicia's Life

How do parents find the strength, the will, or the energy to go about making arrangements for their beloved child's funeral? The thought of doing so was unthinkable and vastly too painful for me to contemplate. But I have felt my entire life that I am on a spiritual journey in search of greater love and truth, and in order to attain these things, we must overcome our fears.

I believe fear keeps us from finding spiritual fulfillment and self-actualization. My approach to overcoming fear has always been to confront head-on those very things that I fear most. But the one lingering fear that has haunted me throughout adulthood is the thought that something terrible will happen to one of my children. I have never feared for my own safety, yet I have always felt a deep obligation to protect my precious children. Now here I was face-to-face with my worst imaginable nightmare, and I had to cope with the aftermath of this daunting personal tragedy. Confronted with the upcoming service, I had to find meaning in a ritual that would honor and celebrate my daughter's precious life, a life that had been taken far too soon. The confusion, the pressure, the pain, the very thought of doing this were unbearable. I prayed fervently for strength and guidance. It surely came.

In the intense stages of early grief, everything seems unreal. At times, it all felt distorted and dreamlike. During these times, emotional numbness would set in and I would feel removed from the terrible reality that had consumed my life. The phases of grief fade in and out; one minute you're caught in the midst of a powerful wave that threatens to drown you in its destructive force, the next you're reminiscing and laughing about a happy memory of your loved one. The surreal nature of it all helped to ease the burden and allowed me to function. It provided an escape from the unbearable pain, at least for a short while.

It was during this reprieve that we were able to think through and plan the funeral arrangements. Our dear friends gently guided us through the steps we needed to take. We had gone through this with my brother and his family when they had tragically lost their fifteen-year old son, Gabriel, on January 12, 1991, in a car crash. But the thought of going through this excruciating ritual to eulogize and honor my daughter's life and death was unfathomable. Thank God for loving friends and family!

Alicia lived in San Francisco, shared an apartment with four other flight attendants in Boston, and grew up in Ohio. Meanwhile, we lived in Michigan. Where would we hold the funeral service? Most of our family and many wonderful friends lived in Ohio, so we had a location. As it turned out, we not only held a memorial service in Urbana, Ohio but also attended services in New York City, Boston, and Michigan and via telephone in San Francisco. Our dear friends from the Urbana area volunteered to find a location for the service and help with the arrangements. We would have the visitation at the Walter-Schoedinger Funeral Home (which generously offered its services gratis) in Urbana, where we had our nephew Gabriel's funeral; it was the very place where seventeen-year-old Alicia had sung a heartrending *a capella* version of "Amazing Grace" to honor her cousin. She had an angelic voice.

The visitation was set for Sunday evening, September 16, from 4:00 to 8:00 p.m. But, we hadn't counted on the outpouring of love and compassion that would come our way, or the crowd of friends and family who would grace us with their presence. Just as I had dreamed the night before Alicia's murder, friends, acquaintances, loved ones, extended family, teachers, and community members lined up around the block and waited for hours to pay their tribute and honor Alicia. We greeted and hugged a couple thousand people and stood there to receive them for more than eight hours. The only break we took was when an FBI agent made it known that he needed to talk with Bev and me immediately. My defiant side initially resisted, but I relented to give him five minutes. I swore that if he rubbed me the wrong way, I would walk out of the conversation. How dare they interrupt us at a time like this! Thankfully, he turned out to be more humble and considerate than I had expected. His visit was part of their investigation, but his timing was atrocious. I would learn later how inept the FBI, CIA, NSA, and various government leaders had been in their attempts—or lack thereof—to prevent the very preventable tragedy of the September 11 attacks.

We were exhausted after the visitation. One thing that helped me through came from my soft-spoken younger brother, Bob. When he came through the visitation line and we embraced, he said gently but with deep conviction, "With each person that comes through and each hug received, you can gain strength from them and give them some of your pain. That is why they are here." I did so, and was deeply thankful to receive so much love, so much caring, so much compassion, and so much concern. This was what I had witnessed in my dream. This was God's love in action.

The memorial service was set for Monday, September 17. Sandy had helped us find a beautiful Victorian bed and breakfast outside of town, a place where our immediate family, along with Alicia's boyfriend and one of her dear friends, could be with us to face the daunting task ahead. Greg and Lyndsey had flown in from San Francisco and would be a source of strength and support in the days to come. The location for the service, Messiah Lutheran Church, was chosen to accommodate the huge turnout expected. They, like the funeral home, the limousine service from a neighboring town, and many community members, were extraordinarily generous in donating their services to help us mourn our daughter's loss with our family and friends. We gathered together at the B&B for the dreaded journey and traveled in silence in the stretch limo for the short ride to the church.

As we arrived, a multitude of friends and family greeted us. The media was there, but we had no desire to talk with them. Fortunately, my older brother, Bill, has the gift of gab, and he answered their questions with our blessing. The church was overflowing. Some have said there were over 500 people present; several had to stand throughout the lengthy service. My niece, Stephanie, had connected us with a dancer who would perform a soulful, ethereal dance choreographed for a song written by another very talented friend of ours, Lisa. Her flowing white gown and graceful movements were angelic and very apropos for the occasion. Alicia loved dancing. When she was a little girl, we would dance for hours, her in my arms, laughing and feeling life's joy. For awhile she had the nickname "Boogie." She always retained her love of dancing and would go out dancing with her friends, often staying to boogie all night.

Throughout the service we incorporated music that held special meaning for us and Alicia. Alicia's piano teacher from her preadolescent years graciously agreed to play a song at the service. The song we chose was "Let There Be Peace on Earth, and Let It Begin with Me." We sought to convey to the world that we did not want our daughter's death to be the cause of more violence, more hate, more killing of innocent people.

To honor Alicia as she had honored her cousin Gabe, our son Zac sang "Amazing Grace." His tenor voice rang out clearly with courage and conviction until he came to the second verse. I could see the grief crash down on him. As if it had been rehearsed, everyone in the church picked up where he had hesitated, but only for a few lines, until Zac took over again with renewed strength and purpose. It was very moving. It touched my soul.

The memorial service message came from many of us, but the crux of it came from three Swedenborgian ministers and a lay minister who had adored Alicia. Their messages were rich with stories of Alicia, messages of love and understanding of the mysteries of life and death, and visions of hope that can only come from a wise and loving God. Each of them knew Alicia and our family personally, and their messages filled our hearts and soothed our souls. My own tribute was short but heartfelt; I felt the need to honor the Alicia's peaceful nature. Following are my words, which were delivered through tears and deep pain. These were the words that would guide me to become an advocate of peace, forgiveness and reconciliation.

We all knew Alicia and loved the person she was and still is. She was always up-front with her true self: stalwart, forthright, honest, and genuine. Yet her greatest gifts were about peace, love, joy, and life itself. Each day she lived life to the fullest and managed to pack a lot in her short twenty-eight years and three months. She wasn't striving for martyrdom, but as the years unfurl, it will be compelling to place her there. She gave so much and was always such a gentle, true spirit.

It's not coincidental or happenstance that Alicia was onboard United Flight 175. Her whole existence on this plane led to her presence, that fateful day, on that plane. She totally opposed violence, acts of terrorism, hate, prejudice, killing, or any malicious act against another living thing. Her true nature and human existence were totally opposite of the evil forces that took her life.

My family, friends and I have reminisced and shared much in the last few days. And one thing that we all agree on: Alicia did not sit passively while this was going on. I can see her trying to talk some sense into the perpetrators, or protecting the little ones from harm, or soothing the hysterical passengers who needed comfort, or trying to organize a resistance movement. Alicia died attempting to do good in the midst of evil.

So why was Alicia on Flight 175 that morning? After all, she had tried to change her schedule to be home with us on that day, to help us care for her nephew, Logan, whom she loved with all her heart. My longtime friend, Reverend Dr. Dorothea Harvey, called me up the other day and said, "It was not accidental that Alicia was aboard that flight. She was there for a purpose to serve. She made this supreme sacrifice because her soul was strong enough to handle the tragic shock of dying by such a violent and outrageous act of hate and evil. And she was there because she could help others in the transition. Her soul will not linger in confusion due to this. God was with her the whole way."

I believe this with all my heart. I look back at her life, her strength, the depth of her love, her compassion for others, her joie de vivre, her childlike innocence, her playful nature, her sense of peace, her exuberance, her quest for truth… And I find comfort in the fact that she did not die in vain.

Her message will be heard. What she stood for will be proclaimed by many and shared for generations to come. All of us who knew and loved her are the ones who will make this happen. We have been blessed with the gift of Alicia and our calling is to assure that her message is heard throughout the land: Love and understanding are the only way to overpower hate and misdirection.

And while we all would agree that these violent acts of terrorism, so filled with hate, cannot be allowed, let us not seek to destroy innocent people and sink to the terrorists' level in our attempts to combat this hate and evil. Let God's wisdom prevail and His love overcome. Let not our hearts be filled with vengeful anger, but love and compassion and a sense of justice. For that's what Alicia was all about. And so, I reiterate the words that Jesus prayed while dying on the cross: "Father, forgive them, for they know not what they do."

I wrote a poem for the service and tried to capture Alicia's beautiful spirit. It came to me while meditating and spoke of Alicia's essence:

Soulful beauty, essence of love;
Joyous elation, inspired from above.
Embodiment of spirit so full and pure,
Gentle, sweet nature; always so sure.

Direct with truth, she could not tell a lie,
Taken so young, and God, we implore you, why?
What is the purpose, the meaning, the good,
Of her premature death? not understood.

Her joy, contagious; her heart was grand;
Peace and nonviolence; love thy fellow man.
Do no harm nor cause pain to another;
Her gentle, true spirit came from her mother.

Of late, she blossomed like a beautiful flower;
It seemed so pronounced in her final hour.
At peace with herself and divinely in bloom;
Her laughter, her smile could light up a room.

Her message was clear for the world to know,
Love one another and the feeling will grow.
Forgiveness is divine, often misunderstood;
Peace on earth, always strive to do good.

Bev read the prayer by St. Francis of Assisi, which was found in a book of quotes on Alicia's bedside table, marked with a bookmark. Although Alicia was not a devoutly religious person, she was deeply spiritual and lived her life in accordance with divine principles such as "Do unto others as you would have them do to you" and "Blessed are the peace-makers." She lived her life with a deep understanding of the truth and compassion spoken of in this beloved poem. She knew the wisdom and love that St. Francis speaks of in this special prayer.

Lord, make me an instrument of your peace.
Where there is hatred, let me sow love.
Where there is injury, pardon.
Where there is doubt, faith.
Where there is despair, hope.
Where there is sadness, joy.

O Divine Master,
Grant that I may not seek so much to be consoled as to console,
To be understood as to understand,
To be loved as to love.
For it is in giving that we receive.
It is in pardoning that we are pardoned.
It is in dying that we are born to eternal life.

Alicia was truly an instrument of God's peace, and she demonstrated this fact every day of her life. Her friends often proclaimed that her very presence would light up a room and make the whole atmosphere more joyous. She had a smile, a friend said, "by which to measure all other smiles." She never had a hateful word for others, and her empathy for those in need or those who were suffering was heartfelt and pure.

When Alicia was four years old, we visited San Francisco. She saw a homeless man standing all alone, downtrodden and defeated. She walked over to him and gave him all the money she earned, one dollar, and smiled her beautiful smile. She was an angel-in-training from the beginning of her life on this earth. She was determined to make this world a better place, and she did. But, it doesn't stop there. She is still very active, doing her best to bring about peace and justice, love and understanding; her soul lives on.

Shanoa read a poem by Edna St. Vincent Millay that Alicia had sent to me in an email a few months prior to her death. Perhaps at some level she knew her life would not "last the night."

My candle burns at both ends
It will not last the night.
But ah, my foes and oh, my friends,
It gives such a lovely light!

Her boyfriend, Greg, and dear friend Lyndsey each shared stories and thoughts about Alicia, as did others. We ended the service by joining hands and singing "Let There Be Peace on Earth and Let It Begin with Me." It was an emotional moment, heavily laden with the weight of the violence that had taken Alicia from us and the turmoil that had resulted. The service was a moving tribute that ended on a comical note, which is vintage Alicia. A family friend, Dick, was trying to get people to go to the reception, but he interrupted the final song, which was one of Alicia's favorites, in doing so. Dick had joked around with Alicia and teased her gently since the days he drove her Head Start bus. As he came up on the stage, barking out orders, he lost his balance and fell off the stage. I thought it was probably Alicia's doing; he said later that it felt like someone had pushed him. We laugh about that today.

We had no body to bury. We had no ashes to take with us. All we had was our lifetime of memories of Alicia, brief as it was. The days that followed were torturous. How could we possibly go back to normal lives after our world had been shattered? Soon we would find out, but I dreaded the thought.

Chapter 8

The Mourning After

After the memorial service and once family and friends had gone back to their lives, the emptiness settled in. Over the years, I've lost many people to death—my fifteen-year-old nephew, my father-in-law, best friends, grandparents whom I loved dearly, favorite aunts and uncles, coworkers—but I was not prepared for the pain I was about to face in the days to come.

Grief has a way of consuming your life. It drains your energy, distorts your thinking, destroys creativity, dominates your mind, disrupts your sleep, strains relationships, and threatens to destroy your very being. Many people in our culture don't allow themselves to grieve, and we usually don't allow time for grief to run its course. After a loss, we're given a few days off of work, and then we're expected to stuff the painful feelings down and get back to business. Some people will send cards and tell you they are sorry; others can only offer a programmed response like, "It will get better in time." The expectation is that life goes on, so we too must move on and put it all behind us.

My internal reaction was quite different from societal expectations. I screamed silently, "How can it possibly get better? My daughter has been violently murdered! No, it won't get better." After a couple of weeks, many people just don't bring the topic up anymore; out of sight, out of mind, as if not bringing it up will make it hurt less badly. Perhaps people don't know what to say or don't want to be upsetting. Or maybe it's because they don't allow themselves to feel at such a deeply painful level. By "protecting" ourselves from feeling sadness and pain, we may be thwarting the development of deeper compassion and ultimately stunting our souls' development. I frequently tell people that Alicia is always foremost on my mind. I welcome the opportunity to talk about her and about my pain and my grief. With some people, you can see it in their eyes—the empathy, and understanding. Knowing that I was not alone helped me tremendously.

On September 19, I wrote in my journal:

The past week was like a bad dream, a time warp. Life goes on for most people, but somehow it's at a different cadence than mine. Reality seems so obscure. Time seems to be measured by a different meter. Everything around me, the conversations, the ongoing interactions, the daily grind, all seem so trivial, so mundane, and so nonsensical. Every part of me is hurting from the inside out. My soul feels the searing pain, a loss that only a parent could feel when a child as beautiful in spirit as Alicia has been violently torn from their arms.

Everyone wants to know why. Why Alicia? But I sense, deep within, the answer. I know that God's grace is present in all of this; the meaning and purpose will be found. Clarity will come to those who seek God's love and understanding. I also know that life as it once was will never be the same. The world will be forever changed. The scales of life's precarious balance will be weighted toward love and understanding. Love will conquer hate and the hells will be subdued. Peace on earth, good will toward all mankind shall be strengthened in the midst of chaos and confusion, the hatred and the killing.

I pray, dear God, help me to live as You would will for me. Help me to see clearly, always to seek truth, to love in accordance with that truth, and to do good in a world that has so much pain and suffering. Direct my course, dear God; open my eyes and fill my heart with love and hope. Be with my family and all those who are suffering. Help us to find peace.

Chapter 9

Grief is a Desolate Journey

I took two and a half weeks off of work before I reluctantly decided to go back. Isn't that what we're taught? We must lose yourself in work and routine to avoid thinking about a loss—or we just have to learn to "suck it up" or "tough it out." But neither of those old adages applies when it comes to healing our grief. They only delay the inevitable and prolong the grieving process. Perhaps that is why so many people turn to medication when the going gets tough. I was not going to become an emotional zombie by taking an anti-depressant if I didn't absolutely need to. I was in deep pain. My world had been destroyed. I needed to feel the emotions. I had to try and sort through all of the confusion and heartache. And I needed to find my way through to the other side of this hell without medication. My beautiful daughter had been taken from me because of ugly politics and fundamentalist religiosity. The oversimplified reason given for the terrorists' attacks by our then-president was because they were "evildoers who hate our freedom." Hidden beneath this political rhetoric lay the real truth, which was much more complex and deep-seated than this one-dimensional overview. Political rationalizations and catch phrases for why my daughter was murdered simply were not good enough. I needed to find out the truth and I was determined to do so, even if it took a lifetime.

I lifted my eyes to the heavens in search of comfort and clarity as the political upheaval swirled about me, and I wrote:

As the day fades into the night and my body feels the full weight of my heart's loss, I struggle to hold back the monumental force of my grief. The gaping hole in my heart spills forth the life-force energy within and bleeds profusely until only emptiness remains. My life has been an ongoing effort to develop and manifest the fullness of my love; to give of it freely and unconditionally; and to grow in understanding of God's truth. God has truly blessed me with a loving wife and wonderful children, and my love has grown in leaps and bounds. Now comes a test of all of my efforts toward good as I suffer the painful loss of one of my beloved children, my eldest daughter and my first child born of our love.

I love my children with all my heart. In return, I've learned greater love, gained a greater understanding of life, experienced abundant joy, and felt a deep sense of fulfillment. My soul rejoices in song and resonates in harmony with love in my heart. Now, I search for the chords of truth in the lost echoes of my dear Alicia's song as it fades from my ears. Oh, God. When will this pain subside? How will I ever feel the full resonance of joy once again? Comfort us in our hour of pain and need; and fill our hearts once again with the joy that resounds in the peripheral realms of my soul's longings. Fill my heart with love; my mind with true understanding; and my doing with acts of charity and giving. (Journal, October 22, 2001)

Upon returning to work, I only went through the motions. I would sit mindlessly through meetings about curriculum changes, the capabilities of our computer system, articulation agreements with other colleges, and other "matters of consequence." My mind was far away, and it was hard to focus on things that seemed so removed and trivial in the midst of my life-and-death issues. But I needed to focus. I had just hired some new counselors and other staff and had made changes in our counseling and advising systems that shifted the dynamics significantly. I needed to be fully present and involved, but, I just couldn't do it. Several coworkers, the campus minister, a coworker who was both a professor and a priest, and several compassionate others checked on me on a regular basis. Their care and love sustained me. But things weren't getting any better. My heart hurt more than I could bear. I tried to fool myself into thinking that the situation was improving, but the hurt was deep within my soul.

Back at work after a long weekend. The daily issues considered important and the administrative functions of directing a program all seem so trivial and inconsequential in comparison to my loss. Alicia holds my attention, my thoughts, my feelings, and my energy. My heart aches with a pain that is incomprehensible to those who have not felt such a loss. Joy is but a faraway feeling that seems to fade more each day.

Yesterday Alicia came to me while I was meditating in the serenity of the early morning. Her changes were apparent, with her true essence shining forth like a white light from her golden features. Her angelic presence radiated through her loving smile, and her genuine love warmed my soul. She was in the presence of the Divine, and the Divine was within her. Her journey here in this life, the profound lessons learned, the many acts of kindness and good deeds, *the depth of love she had developed in conjunction with her ever-changing and expanding understanding of truth, all contributed to her regeneration. Her journey and the sacrifice of her life so that others might grow in peace, justice, love, compassion, and truth all helped her develop her true essence for her journey beyond life, her deserved status in heaven.*

Alicia was on a mission to make a difference in a profound and meaningful way. And she did. Her message will live in the hearts of all those people who have been touched by her in some way. Her light will continue to shine forth, bringing hope for peace and love in our hearts, God willing. Now we must go forth and make it so. Dear God, may thy will be done on earth as it is in heaven. I love you, Alicia. (Journal, November 26, 2001)

At home, the emotions were intense and the tension was thick. Bev and I were both emotionally and physically worn out, and most of the time we were at our wits' end. The constant onslaught of painfully intense feelings is hard to identify, let alone express; communication falls apart. We just wanted some relief from it all.

My journal became a place where I could process my thoughts and feelings, an escape from the haunting pain. I wrote whatever came forth, a strategy that proved very cathartic. I wrote about God, about life and death, and about love and loss. I was always searching for answers.

The mystery of life unravels in my relentless pursuit for clarity of mind and the solemnity of peace to fill my soul. I search for answers to questions not fully formulated, and I long for understanding of that which I could not possibly understand. I implore God to enlighten my soul and for comfort in the midst of this heart-wrenching pain. I search for peace in the heat of the battle that rages all around me. I peer into the face of the Great Mystery and search for light to brighten my way. I cry out in desperation for release from this dreadful nightmare. And I search beseechingly for my deceased loved one, but, only her memory graces my mind. The essence of her joyous soul is somewhere in the great beyond. I reach out for her gentle hand and cry out when in its place comes the cold night wind. I longingly ask for one more embrace and the chance to tell my sweet Alicia how dear she is to me. I want only a chance to kiss her cheek; to gently caress her soft, fragrant hair; to surround her with a father's protection and keep her safe from harm.

My heart feels as if it will burst from the loneliness. Somehow, life goes on around me as I shuffle ahead with my slumped head and my weary old legs. I search the eyes of the faceless people going about their absurdly routine tasks, etched in mundane emptiness, striving for meaningless results. And life goes on. The absurdity of my own trivial pursuits and apparently inconsequential goals smirks at me as I will myself toward normalcy and equilibrium. The surreal experience of my existence vividly portrays the illusion I have created. My world is suddenly upside down, and I am lost in my attempt to make sense out of the extreme craziness that took the life of Alicia and so many other innocent people.

God, be with us all as we strive for justice and peace. May our prayers be heard. May the hearts of all people be filled with your love and our eyes opened to your light of truth. Guide our hands as we reach out to one another in a genuine attempt to embrace our brothers and sisters throughout the world. Amen. (Journal, October 21, 2001)

In early days after Alicia's death, we relied heavily on loved ones to help us through. They rose graciously to the occasion. We reminisced about Alicia: funny memories filled with laughter, proud memories of achievement, loving memories with meaning and purpose, sad memories because that was all we had left of her now. That's so important in grief—to reminisce lovingly about the lost one's life and how it impacted each of us. Someone at work sent me a handwritten card shortly after I returned on which they had written, "Your memories are the bridge that connects you to your deceased loved one." I found comfort in that thought and tacked the card on my wall. It is still there. I yearned for memories so that I could feel that connection and bring my dear Alicia to life in my mind.

As time went on, family and friends drifted from view. Only a few remained, and they helped us tremendously in our time of desolation and need. After the allotted grieving period, family members and friends go back to their day-to-day routines. They don't have a clue whether they can help or what they can do. At times, we felt abandoned by those we had envisioned would be there for us indefinitely. We didn't have any choice but to trudge onward through the heartache and try to make it through the drudgery of each new day. They did.

People in our culture don't often relate well to one another at a deep, meaningful level. We often avoid important or upsetting issues. We do know how to talk about all the latest gossip, football heroes, television nonsense, and the latest in non-meaningful events. But there is no escape from grief's daunting pursuit. The only way to deal with grief is to go through its very heart; to feel the painful feelings; to cry the tears of sadness; to relive those precious moments of bygone days, now mired in pain; to strive to understand the confusing and often irrational thoughts that abound. I also realized that I needed to renew my relationship with God and find peace in my soul. I couldn't go through it alone, but I had to—or so it seemed. Grieving people need help sorting out the confusing and complex changes that loss brings. We need each other more than ever during these times, and we need to feel the interconnectedness of all life at a deep and meaningful level. We need to feel the presence of God through the compassion of others. Grief provides opportunities to reconnect and to reach out to one another in our time of need. Looking back, we and our loved ones missed opportunities to further develop our relationships. This saddens me.

I worked through the winter and into early spring. The daily routine became toil, even though everyone at work was wonderfully supportive. My supervisor told me that, if I needed some extra time at lunch or any time off at all, I should just take it. My position didn't present a lot of demands and expectations beyond the normal daily routine, but it felt overwhelming nonetheless. The College even held a very moving memorial service for Alicia, attended by a few hundred coworkers, after I had been back to work for a couple of weeks. I couldn't have asked for a more supportive work environment. But I soon realized that it wasn't "getting better," and I knew from my formal education in counseling and my current reading about grief that it was going to take time to come to grips with my daughter's death and move on with my life. What I was experiencing was a form of situational depression: my sleep patterns were disrupted, I couldn't concentrate on work or anything else, I was deeply sad and cried a lot, and I had no interest in doing much of anything. I have described it as a sensation of spiraling downward into a deep, dark abyss—and I wasn't sure whether I could find my way back out if I sank too far into its depths.

Chapter 10

Amazing Grace

Shortly after the memorial service in Urbana, we had to find the time and energy to go to Boston and retrieve Alicia's personal effects at her shared apartment. We also needed to go to her apartment in San Francisco and make arrangements to find new homes for her furniture and figure out how to transport the rest of her earthly possessions back to our home in Michigan. Her San Francisco apartment had to be cleared out before the end of the month.

In mid-September we were invited to a special service in Boston commemorating the crews on American Airlines Flight 11 and United Airlines Flight 175, the planes that flew out of Logan International Airport on September 11 and struck the North and South Towers of the World Trade Center. United would fly us there and take care of all our arrangements. During our trip to Boston, we had a remarkable experience, which I described in my journal.

While waiting at Detroit Airport, en route to Boston for the memorial service by way of Washington, D.C., a group of youth with an animated leader was talking in excited, yet subdued tones. The leader, a black youth, came over to me and asked if I could sing. I told him yes, so, he asked if I would sing his mother's favorite song, "Amazing Grace." He explained that he and his buddies were on their way to Fort Benning, Georgia for basic training. They had just joined the Army and he was feeling scared, so he needed to hear a gospel song. I explained that I would have loved to sing, but my heart was broken—I had just lost my daughter. I told him that it had been her favorite spiritual as well. I also shared with him that my son Zac had sung this song at Alicia's memorial service a few weeks earlier, and that Alicia had sung it at my nephew Gabe's funeral service when she was seventeen. "I don't think I can get through the song without breaking down," I told him. He apologized profusely and went back over to his friends.

On the airplane, I noticed that Stefan, the young man I had talked with, had an empty seat beside him, so I went back and sat with him for a while. I told him about Alicia—how she had died, how she lived her life with zest and zeal—and I showed him some photographs of her. He told me his story and how he was going into the Service for his country and to make his mama proud. I wished him well and returned to my seat.

The airplane landed at D.C.'s Dulles Airport, and as I walked down the jetway, I approached Stefan and his friends. I told him that Bev and I would sing a verse of "Amazing Grace" for them. They gathered around and listened with reverence and appreciation. After the song was over, they thanked us profusely and headed off to face the unknown—an especially ominous unknown, with the possibility of war looming in this extremely volatile time. Healing love, God's love, was strongly present in that moment. Stefan and his friends had been directed to us for that very purpose. Thank you, dear God. (Journal, October 25, 2001)

The service was held outside near the Boston Commons and was attended by 20,000 people. Everyone treated us like dignitaries: they flew us first-class, put us up in a wonderful hotel, had a car pick us up, took care of our eating arrangements, and demonstrated endless compassion and understanding throughout. The tragedy had been a major loss for the airlines as well, and we felt honored and privileged to be there. But the searing pain remained.

When we had arrived in Boston, we had met several family members of the flight crew members who had perished. It is amazing how powerful the bond is among people whose loved ones were murdered together and shared their last moments on this earth with each other. Words are not needed; expressions, hugs, shared tears, and a rare intensity of empathy transcend all words. We were forever bonded as the souls of our loved ones soared together into the world beyond.

We talked and commiserated with the family members at the hotel. Then we all followed, sheeplike and docile, as we were led to the buses that would take us to the site of the service at the Boston Commons. The service was very powerful and well thought out. I remember hearing uplifting words from clerics of the Christian, Jewish and Muslim faiths. Bagpipers played "Amazing Grace." Each crew member from Flights 11 and 175 was recognized with pictures and representative uniforms. A coworker read the epitaph for each of the fallen as they released a white dove into the heavens in his or her memory. After all of the doves had been released, they joined together in formation, returning from their individual routes out over the Boston Harbor as Bette Midler sang "Wind Beneath My Wings."

The highlight for me was when a string ensemble from the Boston Symphony played a beautiful waltz. I closed my eyes and let the music take me away. Then, like magic, Alicia came to me in a white flowing gown and a radiance that was beyond this world. We were in an elegant, ballroom-like lodge with open walls that led out onto a deck overlooking the mountains and valleys below. We were the only ones there, and we were dancing. Alicia beamed her effervescent smile; I felt peace, serenity, and a clear message that Alicia was with God. As the music came to an end, we danced out on the veranda, and Alicia drifted away with a smile and an assurance that she had made the transition smoothly and her soul was alive and well. This was more than a dream. What I had just experienced was beyond human understanding, perhaps a glimpse into eternity and a message from the Great Mystery beyond. I had been blessed by this powerful moment and my soul felt the healing power of that love, the understanding of life and death, and the mysteries of the heavenly realm.

Other speakers and musicians performed, but I was still reeling from my experience. I looked around at the thousands of souls who had come to grieve with us, and I felt the loving energy that surrounded us as we loaded the buses for the return trip to the hotel. What I had just experienced was the healing power of God and the life of Alicia in the great beyond.

The next morning, we headed to San Francisco and the dreaded task that lay ahead.

Chapter 11

San Francisco and Alicia's Apartment

We arrived in San Francisco, and Greg picked us up at the airport. It was obvious that he was in a lot of pain. Both he and Alicia had been recovering from deeply hurtful relationships when they came together. Neither one had wanted to "get involved" until they were ready, but love doesn't wait: they fell in love despite their caution. We had seen it coming when they joined us for our family vacation in the Thousand Islands near Gananoque, Ontario, in July of 2001, the last time we would see Alicia alive. It was a wondrous and, in retrospect, dreamlike time: the magic of being on Hay Island and staying in our dear friends' cottages; the time together just relaxing, reading, sailing, eating... We had visited this magical place annually as a family for twenty years. Bev and I had just renewed our vows there a couple of years prior, with Alicia and our other children standing up with us, my dad performing the service, and over thirty family members present. It was a place of serenity and peace, where relaxation was the only demand, where familial love flourished.

Coming to San Francisco was incredibly difficult. We were excited to see Greg, but the nervous anticipation of what awaited us and the gravity of the moment kept us in silence for much of the journey to Alicia's apartment. As we approached her apartment we saw that the neighbors had placed, in front of her building, a lit memorial candle, pictures of Alicia, and heartfelt messages of hope and grief together with flowers and memorabilia. We walked through the huge wooden front door into the marbled foyer and climbed the flight of stairs to the apartment. With each step, my heart grew heavier.

Streams of tears flowed down our cheeks as we opened the door to what had been Alicia's home for three years. The smells, the decor, the colors she had chosen for the walls, the furniture, her personal items, her many books in various locations, her bed with a starfish on the wall above, the view of the San Francisco hills, and the painting "Flaming June" gracing the wall of her living room: all created the odd and momentarily joyous sensation that Alicia was there. I can't begin to express the myriad emotions that erupted within: a lifetime of glorious memories; the intense pain of loss; the deep and heartfelt love we felt for our daughter; and the bottomless sadness that pervaded. It was more than a heart should have to bear. It was a power so strong, so pervasive, so destructive, that we felt helpless in its face. All we could do was weep. *God, give us strength to carry on,* I fervently prayed.

The task ahead left us feeling hopeless, distraught, and helpless in the face of its magnitude and intensity. Every part of me resisted vehemently what we had to do: to dismantle Alicia's life, to undo all that she had so thoughtfully created, to destroy the nest she had built for herself. I couldn't do this. I did not want to do this. Why, dear God? Why Alicia? Why did this have to be?

After our first night in Alicia's apartment, I wrote her a letter:

Dear Alicia,

I awoke more at peace than on the previous morn. I feel the serenity in your soul as you return home to familial souls in heaven. The joy and exultation you must feel is beyond words as you enter your heaven with the angels, whose love and understanding align with yours. What a beautiful and joyous place this must be!

I miss you so much, my dear, sweet Alicia. I feel your essence here among your earthly possessions. I smell your fragrance. I see the laughter on your beautiful face when I close my eyes. I thank you for blessing us all with your angelic presence here on earth. This world was not ready for someone as soulfully beautiful as you.

Before you blessed us with your earthly presence, I was a lost soul with an undefined mission in life, searching for truth, love, and happiness, when you blessed us with your presence, your birth. Your mom and I, both of us were struggling; searching, longing for love; stumbling toward truth; when, lo and behold, you came to us. God had truly blessed us. You taught us how to love beyond ourselves. Your presence brought God back into our lives, and your example challenged us to become better parents and better people. You were and still are God's messenger, sent to direct our course and show us the way. In many ways you outgrew us, but the path is now illumined with your love.

Thank you for our last dance at the memorial service in Boston on Wednesday. It was so glorious, so emblematic of your spirit: the symphonic sounds; the open ballroom; the balcony overlooking the valley below and the ostentatious mountains; the graceful, flowing dance as we drifted effortlessly across the floor. All seemed so real, so wonderful with your beaming face and joyous laughter, your appearance in the flowing white dress adorned like a bride in waiting, and your graceful exit, a culmination of a life well-lived. Thank you for that special moment and for the confirmation that your soul is in its place and all is well with you.

You touched so many lives with your sweet and innocent charm, your bold and adventurous journey here on earth, your loving and peaceful nature, your open embrace for all people, and your exuberance for life itself. Most people could only wish for one day of such glory; you had twenty-eight years and three months. God blessed us with your presence. (Journal, September 27, 2001)

We savored every moment we could of being in Alicia's space just as she had left it. We had a few days, and we weren't about to disrupt what little comfort we could grasp by just being there in her domain. In the meantime, we had to assess systematically how we were going to proceed, what we would take back home with us, what to give away, whom to give it to, and the logistics of doing all these things we so dreaded. It was mind-boggling. Life was mind-boggling. And every part of me resisted what we had to do.

Alicia's friends invited us to join them for an "Alicia" evening out. We would go out to eat at one of her favorite restaurants, join more friends at a pub, and go to her favorite nightclub, an art museum that served as a dance club in downtown San Francisco. We met her friends, the highlight of the evening, but even though the evening was ripe with potential for fun and excitement and in keeping with Alicia's spirit, it was too much. I felt as if I were going to explode inside.

As I sit waiting to dine at the table with Alicia's San Francisco friends, I was torn by the love that surrounded me and the grief in my heart. A part of me was missing. The love from those around me comforted me, but there was a gaping hole that had once been filled with sweet Alicia's presence. The wonderful people surrounding me had so much love in their hearts for Alicia, and our collective pain was immense.

The evening was supposed to unfold with a journey of nostalgic memories on the path she once traversed, but the emotions were swirling around me with the force of a tornado. I could feel Alicia's spirit, but it seemed distant because I couldn't see her, or embrace her. Alicia's friends were wonderful, but the vital centerpiece was missing. So we called it an evening, and Greg drove us to Alicia's apartment. We would keep in touch and become friends ourselves with several of her friends as time moved on. For now, we just needed to retreat and mourn.

As the evening came to a close, I closed my tearful eyes and said a prayer to Alicia:

Find peace, my gentle lamb. Take your rightful place among the heavens: a place where truth is pure and never obscured, a place where joy abounds, a place where a soul as beautiful as yours can flourish and grow with kindred souls, a place where God's will is not obliterated by human self-serving wills, a place where magnificence and true beauty abound and peace is in the hearts of everyone, a place where righteousness and justice are in accordance with God's order. You are home now, sweetheart. You are sadly missed by us all. The depth of our love for you is fathomless. Someday, we will once again join you and your spiritual family. Although you are gone from our eyes, your flame still burns brightly in our hearts, and your face manifests the richness of your spirit in our minds. I miss you, honey. (Journal, September 27, 2001)

Back at the apartment, we started going through Alicia's private possessions, reading her journals and looking for confirmation of her life, painstakingly searching for memories to cling to. Everything seemed so unreal, like something from a distant past that was too painful to acknowledge. We ran the gauntlet of the emotional onslaught, everything from out-of-control sobbing to an apparent calm that was really only an emotional hiatus. Occasionally, we would be reminded of something humorous and let out a laugh that seemed distant and foreign.

The sorting and boxing of Alicia's possessions was very laborious and painstaking, and the process was compounded by the emotionality of it all. We made arrangements to give some of her furniture to a friend, Michelle, even though we didn't really want to give anything away. Later, we would share many of her clothes and other possessions with family and friends back home. Everyone wanted a memento to cherish and remind them of her. Bev latched onto her pillows. They have given her comfort on many nights and still do. At first, we could smell Alicia on her pillowcases and clothing, but, like the memories of the last time we'd held her, laughed with her, or talked with her, that too faded away.

Finally, after three days of packing, we had everything ready to go. We leased a rental truck to haul the forty boxes to the airport. United Airlines had generously offered to ship her possessions back for us once we got them to the airport. We gave parting hugs to Greg, Lyndsey, and Tamara and boarded the United Airlines jet. Once again, the flight crew treated us like royalty. The painful recognition on their faces and the compassion in their eyes spoke of their own grief and fear. We had just put behind us another chapter in this saga, but we carried unresolved emotions and painful memories with us.

Life was barely tolerable in the days that followed. The waves of grief crashed down upon us like tsunamis, wreaking havoc on the shores of our reality and devastating our dreams. People showered us with cards, gifts, and genuine sympathy. Their generosity restored our faith in humankind, but the pain grew with each passing day as the memories of Alicia's life became ever more distant and abstracted. How I longed to hold her in my arms just one more time!

United Airlines offered to continue our benefit of free standby travel, one of the benefits that came with Alicia's employment. We took advantage of the perk as we traveled to California, Montana (to visit Zac and Lana), New York, Canada, and eventually Italy. It was better than staying at home and drowning in our sorrow. Like Alicia, we loved to travel, but in many ways the thrill was gone. Everything seemed to be diminished and artificial.

I wrote a prayer in my journal that typified my confusion and my pleas for solace:

The voyage I am on has surely been a "road less traveled" and fraught with peril. I know that pain and suffering can empower my soul and strengthen my convictions; I know that the greater the love I give, the greater the pain of my suffering in loss; I know also that, in my finite and limited mind, I cannot possibly understand the profundity and full ramifications of the tragedy that has befallen us. So I pray for clarity of mind and seek solace for my broken heart. Help guide my way in this world devastated by evil and hate. Help me forgive my enemy and reach out to my neighbor. Give me strength for the sake of goodness, love, and truth. Bring peace to us all and help us, once again, to feel joy in our hearts. Amen. (Journal, October 2001)

Chapter 12

Ground Zero

In October of 2001, we were invited to a memorial ceremony at Ground Zero, the site of the World Trade Center. Attending were dignitaries, religious leaders from the major religions, musicians, renowned singers like Andrea Bocelli and Renée Fleming, politicians who came for mixed reasons, and thousands of grieving family members who had lost loved ones on September 11. All the arrangements had been made. United Airlines arranged our flight and other aspects, including a dinner with Alicia's supervisors and coworkers. They all spoke very highly of her and related "Alicia stories" that were inspirational, uplifting, and frequently humorous. Zac and Lana flew in from Montana and met the family of a young woman, Lisa Frost, who had just graduated from Boston College. She was an amazing young lady who had lived a rich life filled with heartfelt service and giving to others in her twenty-two years. She sounded a lot like Alicia in many ways. When we met them, we had an instant bond, a "knowing" at the soul level, a sharing of something so unique and painful that it transcended all mundane and superficial communication. When I hugged Lisa's father, we sobbed together like long-lost friends. It was a hug many men will never allow themselves to experience.

We met many other grieving hearts along the way: a father wearing his fireman son's uniform, siblings who had lost a brother or sister, parents, spouses, friends, coworkers, and others. Everyone wore that all-too-familiar look of distress and pain. Hearing their stories and learning about their loved ones made me realize the cataclysmic effect of the 9/11 tragedy on the collective soul of America and all of humanity. It also helped me see the power of unchecked evil and the need for goodness and truth to be made actively manifest in all of God's creation.

Goodness cannot remain passive, for the nature of evil is to destroy all that is good and true. Love and truth must be put to use for the good of all. They cannot exist in a vacuum.

On the morning of the service, we walked from our hotel to Ground Zero. The rancid smoke still pouring from the ruins, the mournful looks on people's faces, the air of death, and the charred ruins reminded me of a concentration camp. Security was tight; tension was high. I felt as if I were entering a war zone. The stage for the performances and speakers overlooked the devastation, and five thousand chairs had been placed around it. There was a huge problem, however; the number of people attending must have been fifteen to twenty thousand. We didn't feel like fighting the crowd, so we positioned ourselves about a quarter of a mile from the ceremony. It was a horrible experience. Remote speakers had been set up, but the whole scene reeked of death and destruction; our daughter's ashes, along with our own hearts were among the still-burning debris. We had to retreat before the ceremony was over. We were completely overwhelmed.

On the way back to the hotel many greeted us along the way; homeless people gave us full eye contact and empathetic looks and told us they were sorry for our loss. New York City was reaching out to us with true emotion, with sympathy and understanding, with affirmation and hope—not something I had expected.

In an attempt to lighten our load we took the family out to the Broadway show *The Full Monty*. It helped briefly, but our efforts to alleviate the pain were only stopgaps. We were reminded once again that there was no escape from the loneliness and all-encompassing grief.

Being in New York City so soon after the attacks had proven to be too much, too soon. At some level, though, it probably aided in our healing. After all, Alicia's ashes were part of the devastation and ruin, but her soul was with the angels. I am sad for those who do not believe in life after death. For me, it's not a matter of being able to prove the existence of God and a spiritual world. My belief in life after death is as much a part of who I am and what I know to be true as life itself.

It's a rainy overcast day outside—and within my heart as well. As the reality of our loss takes root in my conscious mind, the consequent searing pain tugs at my heart strings. After visiting the stark devastation of what used to be the World Trade Center this past weekend, listening to the heart-wrenching stories from the families of the other victims, and crying with them while praying for peace and healing love, I found myself back in a whirlwind of emotions that I had hoped had subsided. Yet I felt a compelling need to visit the site and share with others in our collective grieving.

Grieving is a personal journey that unfolds differently for each of us, but sharing with others helps to ease the burden and lighten the load. So many people have reached out to us with loving concern! For that, I am eternally grateful. This is healing power and goodness from God that has been bestowed upon us. I continue to give thanks throughout this trying time for my many blessings, and especially for having had Alicia in my life for 28 years. She was such an inspiration, a spirited and joyous young lady who filled my heart with love and laughter. Her zest for life; her gentle, sweet nature; her quest for understanding; her bold, adventurous walk through life; and her lifelong journey of love and search for fulfillment all spoke of a life well-lived. Her memory will serve as a source of hope for us all when the journey becomes too arduous and the load too burdensome.

As we cry our tears of sadness and feel the deep pain of our loss, let us rejoice for the many blessings in our lives and for the joy that longs for expression as life continues to reveal its glory and mystery. May we reach out to each other with loving hands, sing like the early-morning birds as they greet the dawning of a new day, take time to savor the sweet smells of the beautiful flowers, laugh at humorous things, and enjoy the moment in its fullest, for this is what God intends for us, and this is the essence of Alicia. (Journal, November 2, 2001)

The days that followed were stark and desolate. Loneliness, deep pain, an overwhelming feeling of despair, and the need for loved ones to help us bear the load was becoming more pronounced. It was such a confusing time in life; on one hand, we longed to run away, to isolate ourselves from all of the craziness and avoid having to deal with the shallowness that seemed so prevalent in people's daily lives. On the other hand, however, we needed to know that our friends and family were with us on our grief journey. A faithful few reached out to us regularly. It was as if they knew intuitively what we needed: a brief email expressing their love, a card with the words "thinking of you," a phone call to convey their love to us, or a genuine question like "How are you doing?" that opened the door for an honest response. But what really stood out were the people who did not call, or, if they did, merely talked around the real issue of Alicia's death and our suffering, simply circumventing the "elephant in the room."

It is difficult for people to know what to do at a time like this. Each of us process feelings differently, and our upbringings usually don't prepare us for how to deal with tragedy and personal loss. I knew this intellectually, but I still felt abandoned by some in my life whom I love and care for very much. Many complete strangers and more distant acquaintances were able to respond to the depth of our pain. Some close to us were uncertain about how to respond to our needs, especially since they were grieving too. Some thought we needed our space, didn't want to overwhelm us with their own grief, or simply didn't know what to do—so they did nothing. I can't begin to express how painful I found this silence in our hour of need. We had to walk alone, or so it sometimes felt. Bev and I learned to reach out to each other in spite of our own insatiable needs and relentless struggle to cope. But an opportunity to grow mutual love and deeper understanding with some of our extended family was lost. God gives us opportunities to grow our compassion for others and learn greater truths through tragedy and suffering such as this, but we have to be willing to reach out and take the risk.

Life seems complex and overwhelming as we face our own destinies along our chosen path. Reality can be a cold slap in the face, devoid of joy and fraught with pain along the way. I yearn to stay in the light of truth and allow God's love to work through my daily deeds. But as we grow, the journey becomes more arduous and the lessons learned more painful to overcome. Forces of evil tempt, deceive, and challenge our resolve, leaving doubt, pain, loneliness, and fear in their wake. Our paths branch along the way; and we make choices that confirm, conform, or confound.

> *Conflicting feelings confuse and abate;*
> *Painful memories in my mind permeate.*
> *Anguish and pain scream for resolve,*
> *And grips the heart for loved one lost,*
> *At such a heart-wrenching cost.*
>
> *Glimpses of joy*
> *And of wonders beyond;*
> *Feelings of love fade away…gone,*
> *Gone like the setting sun,*
> *And arise anew in the awakening of dawn.*
> (Journal, November 27, 2001)

I have talked with people who make losing loved ones sound spiritually joyous and uplifting because the deceased person is now "walking with Jesus" or has been "called home." It seems as if these individuals convince themselves that they should not feel the pain of grief because the loss was all in God's plan. More power to them! But losing my daughter hurt deeply, despite my belief that Alicia was with God and amid the angels. I don't believe for a second that God mapped out a grand plan that included the murder of my daughter. By the grace of God, we are given free will, and in that free will, evil (in other words, self-love) is allowed to manifest alongside divine love and wisdom. But through the temptations presented by evil, love and truth will ultimately prevail, because that is God's will for us.

I also think we have to resolve a loss of this magnitude within our own souls and cope with it through our emotional responses. To act as if all is wonderful and glorious in the face of murder and bereavement goes against our God-given emotional response system, not to mention our human nature. I find great comfort in knowing that Alicia's soul lives on in another reality, that divine love and truth will prevail, and that a tragedy like this, by exposing the face of evil, will ultimately serve the cause of good. But I have to face my feelings and work through them, or they will surely destroy me. Grief, indeed, has the power to destroy us, especially if it isn't dealt with in a healthy way.

Chapter 13

Depression, Loneliness, and Despair

During those first few months of grieving, I felt that I was making progress at some level. But grief is both insidious and relentless. I would soon find out that healing progresses in its own time. Birthdays, holidays, and other commemorative dates or times when family would come together for celebration were all excruciating. During these times, everyone went about their normal preparatory tasks, the children played with their usual blitheness, laughter rang out amid lighthearted conversations, the food was as delicious as ever, and all seemed normal—except for this huge hole in our hearts and the absence of our beloved daughter. The contrast was stunning. As much as I wanted to feel joy and bask in the familial love that abounded at these events, I had to be true to myself. I couldn't bring myself to mask my feelings. I did not want to put on a façade, as so many feel obligated to do when dealing with crises in their lives. For me, my grieving signified the love I felt for my deceased daughter. To put on a face that betrayed these feelings would have been dishonest and dishonorable. I also felt that in order for those around us to know how to help, I needed to convey, as best I could, where I was in my grieving. It is all too easy to cover up, mask, deny, or fake our true feelings, but such pretense keeps our loved ones at a distance and promotes superficiality in relationships. I've witnessed the extremes of this phenomenon in my professional work as a mental health counselor and spent many sessions helping the youth I work with to recognize and process their emotional responses and feelings. It was in the midst of this realization that I wrote:

Oh, pen of my expression, I have been remiss. My mind has struggled to understand the whirlwind of my thoughts and the torment of my emotions. The full force of the ocean of grief has nearly drowned me with its relentless waves and turbulent churning. My mind deceived me into believing that the gaping hole in my heart was actually subsiding, but it was only an illusion designed to lift my spirit and allow life once again to flow through my veins. Now the full force of my pain is made manifest, and the sharp blade of grief's dagger penetrates the underbelly of my soul. The tears stream forth like raindrops in the dark of night. Yet somehow the pain of sorrow makes me feel more alive than the numbness that tries to protect and disguise. Love lost manifests with the same degree of heartache as the joy it once gave, equivalent in its expression of pain and loneliness.

Dare I think that perhaps, in a moment of enlightenment, I could almost grasp why something so tragic, so evil, and so utterly devastating happened? At times, I can almost visualize a higher plane of wisdom that somehow lends understanding of how such an atrocity could be of benefit to the overall good. I can grasp the notion that good and evil exist; that God through grace gives us free will to return to the Source through our own choosing; that we as souls coming into this world might fulfill a purpose that could alter the course of human existence and bring about the mass repentance of other souls in overcoming evil. Through free will, we make choices to fulfill our chosen mission or sacred agreement, even, unbeknownst to the conscious mind, sacrificing during our life on earth. Divine providence guides us toward a greater good, but the choices we make through our own understanding of truth, powered by our ruling love, determine whether we achieve our karmic purpose. The return to our Maker, to the Almighty, to the Source of all understanding, to God, is our ultimate purpose. Through our actions, guided by divine love and wisdom, we affect the whole for good or for evil. The complexity of all of this is beyond the finite mind. But, through prayer, purposeful living, faith in God, living our lives in search of truth, developing our love toward compassion and acts of charity we grow in spirituality, personally and interpersonally; for the good of self is in relation to all of life. (Journal, November 15, 2001)

Autumn and early winter are filled with special occasions and holidays for our family, with Bev's birthday, our anniversary, Thanksgiving, Christmas, and then my own birthday. With the passing of each date, I felt as if I should be able to cope better the next time around. How very wrong I was! In those first few months of grief the shock of our loss protected us from the hopelessness and the sense of painful finality that threatened to consume us. Depression lurked like an evil shadow, waiting for a vulnerable moment to attack. At times it felt like the dark abyss would swallow us, but the light of God and the truth of love always held it at bay. I felt my faith growing even as the painful reality of our loss became more pronounced, like a flower growing in the midst of a barren desert. Time moved on into a new year.

Even though the date has changed and all the well-wishers attempt to lend support and offer hope by saying, "This year can only be better," I somehow can't seem to grasp that alien concept. It still feels like the same old year, with all the pain and sadness still as strong as ever. I am an optimist, but no amount of optimism can bring my Alicia back or fill the empty place in our hearts and at our table during holidays and family gatherings. I am hopeful for our future, but the present reality seems to cast a shadow on my hopes and dreams. It is said that time heals all wounds, but does it really? I think we just learn to live with our losses and the pain seems lessened by comparison, but remains with us at some level. This can be life-transforming, or it can be debilitating. I'm hoping for the former.

The holidays have come and gone, and, although it feels more like a hurdle than a joyous occasion, life moves relentlessly onward. Today is not such a good day. My hope is that life will get better, but I won't count on it until it happens. When and if it does, Carpe diem! Seize the day! For I know that it will not last and grief will once again rear its ugly head; and the pain will consume me like a giant wave, slam me down, rake me across the rocky bottom, and hold me under with its force until the next wave strikes. What does the future hold? I must learn how to ride the waves.

In the meantime, I'm going through the motions of living, and I'm praying for healing. I am thankful for and feel blessed by a loving family and friends and a belief system that consoles me in my hour of need. I don't know what I would do without these; life would seem so utterly hopeless and meaningless otherwise.

So, I will try to have a better new year, to search for new truth to lighten my way and renewed love to give meaning to my existence, to allow new hope to inspire my way, new joy to share with others, and new peace for us all. (Journal, January 3, 2002)

Everything comes under scrutiny in the throes of grief: reality itself, life, death, God. Everything becomes a question of faith and an acceptance of the mystery that seems even more complex and overwhelming. Yet one's internal sense of reality itself becomes obscured, and chaos flourishes. Clarity becomes a distant star in the cloudy night. I prayed for understanding. I longed for hope.

My life has careened out of control. What on earth am I going to do? The question implies that many choices exist; therefore, I am free to do anything on this earth that I am called to do. Whence comes the calling? How do I recognize it to be God's calling when it comes? Through faith and a continual search for God's truth.

I hear the echoes of my calling, but my antennae are not receiving. The answer resonates, but it does not seem feasible, nor is it pragmatic—or so it seems. Somehow, I continue the journey, even though my legs are weary from the increasingly heavy load and my heart aches from suppressing my soul's longing for expression. (Journal-January 11, 2002)

Chapter 14

Good, Evil, and the Political Quagmire

Faith is at times a confounding anomaly, requiring a deep belief in a great mystery that cannot be defined in terms our rational minds fully understand. The infinite cannot possibly be fully perceived by the finite. I see human life and all of life as component parts of this concept we call God. Each of us is a small aspect of the whole. God is within each of us and all of life. But, ever since Eve and Adam ate of the fruit of the tree of knowledge of good and evil, the human sense of self has recognized the omnipotent power of the Divine within us and arrogantly believed that we are its source. Emanuel Swedenborg states that the story of the Fall corresponds to "man in his own selfhood, as he is who believes that he does all things, even good, from himself; and eating from the tree means the appropriation of evil."[4] The garden of Eden symbolizes intelligence.

God gives us the gift of free will. The human ego basks in this sense of power to the point of turning it into a self-serving, destructive force. We rationalize what we do outside of God's wisdom and love as being for the good. We even find scripture in the Bible, the Koran, or other sacred documents to help us justify our dirty deeds; the killing of Alicia and three thousand other innocent victims on September 11, 2001 is one stunning example. Another is the fact that we justify the bombing of homes and villages in Afghanistan or Iraq with the proclaimed intent of killing "terrorists" or "insurgents," yet the outcome is the deaths of thousands of innocent people, many of them children. Our government proclaims loudly that we are doing what is necessary for the sake of peace. Such arrogance! Meanwhile, we the people continue to hide our heads in the sand and blindly accept the spin doctors' tale of woe, waving our flags in celebration and cheering our military victories.

I cannot fathom the reasoning behind such thinking. In my mind, it aligns closely with the irrational thinking that propelled Osama bin Laden and his cohorts to kill Alicia and others. The purported difference, which we declare so loudly and self-righteously, is that terrorists target innocent people and we don't. But, in the end, the Afghani and Iraqi fathers and mothers of the thousands of killed and maimed innocent children categorized as "collateral damage" are left with the same sense of despair and injustice as I am. Many of these grieving families will remain bitter toward the United States of America for the rest of their lives—and the cycle of violence will continue for generations to come. The seeds of hate and vengeance have been planted. Most people support this violent approach out of fear, as our re-election of President Bush confirmed; then they turn a blind eye to the human tragedy and personal suffering that inevitably results from such choices.

I am reminded of the stories from our history books of earlier cultures in which the attitude that "only the strong survive" proliferated; the tribes with the best weapons and the most highly trained killers ruled the day. The same mentality permits the existence of slavery and the commission of other atrocious crimes against our fellow human beings. Such a belief does not come from the teaching of Jesus, Buddha, Mohammed, or any of the enlightened ones who formed the bases for our religions—they told us to love one another. The idea that might is right is merely the human ego's justification of inhumane acts and atrocities against our brothers and sisters out of fear, ignorance, and greed. War is not the pathway to peaceful co-existence. When will we learn the true lessons from Jesus' teachings—that we should forgive, love our neighbors (in the broadest sense of the term), bless the peacemakers, and aspire to humility and childlike innocence? We implore our God to bless America, but what about the rest of our neighbors in our world?

For those of us who struggle with the tenets Jesus gave us (and I include myself in this group), such teachings do not mean that we should sit passively back and allow injustice to flourish or evil to proliferate. They also do not mean that we should blindly accept our government's actions without demanding accountability for them. If we do, it will come back to haunt us. I believe that the concept of karma is legitimate and makes sense even within the realm of Christianity. After all, the Golden Rule, "Do unto others as you would have done to you," certainly carries overtones of this concept. So does Jesus' statement in Matthew 25:40: "What you do to the least of these you do to me." Once we accept that all of life comes from God and is of God, how can we justify the killing of innocent children and declare it necessary in the name of freedom? Our own actions and those we condone through our government that lead to the death and destruction of innocent people's lives and homes will come back to us in some form. Or perhaps they already have.

Bishop Tom Gumbleton, long-time peace activist, made a speech at Schoolcraft College prior to the United States' invasion of Iraq in which he told a story about the thousands of Vietnam vets he has served in his soup kitchen in Detroit. He stated that more Vietnam vets have taken their own lives since the Vietnam War than actually died in combat. He went on to say that when a human being is asked to destroy villages containing innocent people as a part of war, it does something deep within us: it destroys a piece of our soul. I believe I would find it extremely difficult to forgive myself if I had done such a thing.

I have heard the stories of people in Afghanistan and Iraq who lost everything—their entire families, their homes, and everything they had worked for—because of our "smart" bombs, or due to "bad intelligence," or for whatever reason we use to justify these acts of murder and destruction. Friends of ours who are also members of September 11th Families for Peaceful Tomorrows met these people, cried with them, and shared deep, healing love and compassion with them. In our confusing world of politics, otherwise moral people somehow remove themselves from the atrocity of the violence inflicted on fellow human beings, creating rationalizations and statistics that justify these horrendous acts. Personally, I am appalled by such thinking. It hurts my soul because I feel the victims' pain. I hear the echoes of their children's cries. I know their heartache. God help us if we numb our hearts.

If we sense the interconnection of all life, we begin to conceive of justice (a concept very different from vengeance) as being universal and divine. Does it not make sense that what we do to the least of these we also do to ourselves and to God? And if we are a part of God (creative life-force energy, the great mystery, or however you conceive of our creator), does it not make sense that the destructive energy we support will indeed double back upon us? I hope that you do not have to come to this realization through the violent murder of your child. It's a painful lesson to learn, one I would not wish upon my worst enemy.

Too many people see the world with self-righteous indignation, justifying acts of violence and destruction and proclaiming it as God's will. Too many of us view the ongoing battles from afar like a competitive sport, a twisted game, using analytical strategies to counter the opposition while anesthetizing our minds to human suffering and cheering loudly when we destroy the opposition. But the inflated ego is really our own worst enemy. It allows us to rationalize acts that contradict our very nature and all that is of the divine. The ego can be a useful tool in our regeneration; or it can lead us down the path of destruction if allowed to dominate unchecked and fed by selfish love—the root of all evil. Being filled with self-love and making choices from our ego mind alone puts us at odds with the concept of love for the other, voiding us of compassion, empathy, and understanding. Self-love feeds the ego and counters God's love, a selfless love that incorporates wisdom.

I have forgiven those who took Alicia's life, even though I abhor their actions. I do believe firmly that they must be brought to justice and be held accountable for what they did. Forgiveness allows me to let go of the hate and desire for revenge that surely has the power to destroy me if I let it. I believe that in killing another we also destroy a part of our own souls. Our penance is self-inflicted. God does not punish us; we punish ourselves because each dark act carries with it its own destructive ramifications for our souls. And besides, vengeance would not help me to feel better or bring Alicia back to me. Misusing my energy toward revenge out of fear or malice would only hold me back from becoming that which my soul longs to become.

Yesterday, I felt the depth of my loss. My heart is aching as I reminisce about the many wonderful moments I shared with Alicia. The joy she brought into my fractured life; the ability to see life through the eyes of this pure and loving child; the magnificence, the unbounded joy, the pure excitement of life itself, the absolute innocence, the glory, the majesty... and her understanding of truth that she received from the divine, which filled her with a knowledge that God exists and life is good.

What becomes of all the innocence and the heartfelt knowing of what is right and true? How can man twist this so cruelly to commit acts of murder? Is it perhaps that, when we ate of the tree of the knowledge of good and evil, life became fraught with a self-chosen peril? We, as human beings, have the capacity to create our own perceived truths and act in accordance with these truths for good or for evil. We manifest by our own deeds that which we wrongly love, and we strive to fulfill our own perceived sense of destiny from our own free will. On our journey through life, we make choices; we often find ourselves standing at the fork in the road and need to decide which way to go, be it right or wrong. Wrong choices can be rectified; we can repent; better choices and greater understanding can be had. God's continual presence and constant forgiveness help us find our way back to the divine path.

But how can we make sense of outrageous acts of terrorism that destroy the lives of innocent people and tear at the heartstrings of the victims' loved ones? I remember reading that when Jesus was born, evil had developed a real stronghold in this world. The balance of good and evil was shifting toward evil. The world needed an infusion of love and a new way of understanding truth. God sent a pure soul, with a powerful love and a clear understanding of truth, to walk among us and spread the seeds of hope—seeds of hope for a world in which joy of living, love of our fellow man, and clarity of purpose were rejuvenated and rebirthed. This new hope inspired people, filling their hearts with wonder, joy, peace and abundant love; and it came out of the depths of despair, hopelessness, selfishness, and lust that people had created for themselves. The evil forces in power were so threatened by the burgeoning strength of such a pure and holy one that they chose to destroy him to set an example, to demonstrate their worldly potency and eradicate the threat that was undermining their power. Oh, how powerful and yet fearful Pontius Pilate and the others must have felt! They would show the world who was in command by imprisoning and then crucifying the Chosen One. Little did they know that this act of misguided power would forever change the world! Divine love and wisdom will ultimately prevail over ignorance and fear.

The tragic events of September 11, 2001 are incomprehensible to the rational mind. Yet, somehow and in some way, I am certain that goodness will surely overcome the evil that destroyed so many innocent lives; love will return to the hearts of people across the land; love of neighbor and love of God will ultimately replace the self-serving, self-centered love so present in this world prior to this horrendous tragedy. New hope will spring forth, laughter will be heard once again, and people will reach out and embrace their neighbor and join together in peace. The goodness of God will prevail and evil will once again be subdued. We have a long road to travel, but the seeds of hope are eternal.

Dear God, let peace and love ring out like a bell in the silent night and truth shine like a beacon in the blinding fog. (Journal, October 2001).

Chapter 15

Alicia and Divine Presence

In my grief, I questioned everything: my concept of God, the innate goodness or evil within the human soul, life and death, the evolution of the human soul, my purpose in life. And I reexamined every fiber and each aspect of my own life and soul. It is not easy to feel so exposed and unprotected. But what did I have to lose? I had lost something profoundly significant to my essence and my life definition. I had nothing more to lose—or at least that's how it felt. My other children, grandson, wife, and family were and are intimately a part of who I am, and I knew I had to work through the grief for their sakes if not for my own. I also knew that Alicia would want me to live life to its fullest and learn to grow in love and understanding from the painful lessons surrounding her death. She would want me to do all I could to make this world better. I could hear the echoes of her soul resonating within my own. I could feel her abiding love in my heart. And I felt the strength of her love to help me carry on.

Many times during those first months after her death, I experienced Alicia's angelic presence and gazed upon her radiant smile: after a run in the woods, while deep in meditation, during moments when I was able to still my mind, in times of despair and moments of desolation, when I would talk in front of groups of people about peace and nonviolence, during family gatherings, out in nature, while holding my grandson and experiencing the innocence of his love, when I would do the yogic sun salutation that Alicia and I had shared together, and when my soul was tired and ready to give in. At all these times, Alicia was with me.

Was I merely imagining her presence? No. Her presence during those times was so pronounced, so real, that I experienced it with my whole being. I was cautious not to hold onto her or yearn for her presence in a self-serving way. I knew that she had to move on into her new life, and I didn't want to hold her back. She had work to do and a life to live in the heavenly realm. She needed to return to her new home, surrounded by kindred souls who resonated at the same level of spiritual evolution, in the presence of the Divine. Upon death, we all move on to continue the journey we have chosen in this life; eternity allows us to carry on with the life determined by our ruling love here on earth: a self-chosen life of heaven in service of others, or a self-serving life of hell that allows us to play out our selfish desires amongst like-minded spirits who share this as their "ruling love."[5]

Alicia and I are kindred souls. Our spirits were very much aligned with one another in many ways. It's not something that is easily defined, yet it is a knowing that transcends the rational mind and is felt deep within the soul. I imagine it must be like what we experience in the afterlife with those kindred souls in the heavenly society where we will reside after death. This sense of knowing another at a soul level is an interconnection of love and understanding that defies logic and transcends the senses. We are sparks of the Divine. Some of these sparks surely must shine with the same luminescence and resonate at the same pitch. It proved very interesting to live this reality out on this plane of existence as father and daughter, fraught as the relationship is with all of the challenges and personal dynamics that come into play and tend to complicate matters. But during our deep and sometimes contentious discussions, through our sharing of writings and spiritual experiences, in our manifestations of love, during moments of shared compassion and intuitions, and through our similarities in spiritual expression, we both recognized our kindred natures. When I shared a poem with her, she would understand my true meaning; when we were able to move beyond superficial discussions and the limitations of mere words in describing what we knew but could not clearly define, it became obvious that our hearts and souls were on the same page.

Bev and Alicia were very close. Alicia and I would sometimes refuse to give in to the other's point of view even though our perspectives were often the same, and sometimes she needed to differentiate while I had a hard time letting go. Bev and she, meanwhile, became closer and more connected, eventually becoming best friends during Alicia's adulthood. Alicia could tell her anything—and did. When Alicia would call (which was often), I could tell immediately that it was her by Bev's excitement and pure joy. Bev admired the woman Alicia was: her stalwart and dogged approach, her adventuresome spirit, her deep compassion for others, her joie de vivre, her boldness, her wisdom, and, especially her abiding love. Alicia lived the life Bev had been denied, in part, by her circumstances growing up. Alicia loved Bev's soulful nature, her heartfelt compassion for those oppressed and in need, her unselfish giving to others, her nurturing spirit, her steadfast love, and her unadulterated wisdom. I truly loved the way they related to each other. Alicia and I challenged each other in ways that helped us both to grow and evolve in wisdom and understanding; Bev and Alicia complemented each other in ways that nurtured their capacities for love.

It was amazing to watch Alicia interact with her brothers and sister. She was an angelic presence in their lives and a wonderful big sister. I never witnessed any resentment on her part, even though, being the oldest, she had to share us with them. She was the type of older sister that we would all dream of having.

Chapter 16

Peacemaking in a Troubled World

Prior to Alicia's death, I had been involved with an organization at Schoolcraft College called the Season for Nonviolence Committee. The concept originated with the thirtieth and fiftieth anniversaries, respectively, of the deaths of Reverend Dr. Martin Luther King, Jr. and Mahatma Gandhi, two of the most revered peacemakers in modern times whose influence has significantly changed and continues to change our world.

During the fall of 2001, our committee decided to engage local religious leaders in an effort to help the community understand and heal after the September 11 tragedy. We invited clerics and representatives from major religions to speak on forgiveness and peace in relation to the attacks, pulling from the teachings of their religions. Students, faculty, staff, and community were invited. I was hoping that great things would come out of this event, helping to dispel ignorance, enlighten others about the truth and love within each religion, aid in our healing, and, perhaps, reduce some of the underlying fear shaping decisions that ultimately would be used to justify the mass killing of innocent Afghanis by bombing. I had high expectations for these discussions; I was desperately hoping that the local imam would help us all better understand the teachings of Mohammed and his condemnation of the kind of barbaric act that took Alicia's life. I had recently read and listened to taped portions from the Koran to try and discover what Mohammed had said and what Islam was about. But I wanted to know more.

The stage was set and the messages were profound and heartfelt— the message of peace from the Quaker, the Pathway to Enlightenment of the Buddhist, the inspirational message from the Hindu, the concept of divine love and wisdom in our daily lives by a Swedenborgian Christian, and the highly anticipated message of hope from the Muslim. I had talked with the Muslim cleric prior to the program and expressed my thoughts about the healing that could result from his message. Perhaps my aspirations were too high. Perhaps he had mixed feelings of his own. But when students asked him pointed questions about the attacks against America by Islamic extremist Osama bin Laden and others, he was unable to refute convincingly bin Laden's distortions or distance his beliefs from theirs.

I was disappointed. From my limited knowledge of Mohammed's teachings, I could have shown the extreme and false interpretations that were used to justify these murderous acts against America. But, I would soon discover, it goes much deeper than that: years of policies that had resulted in the oppression of Afghanis and others in the Muslim world; arrogant and self-serving decisions by leaders of our country that disrespected the Muslim people and their belief system in Saudi Arabia during the first gulf war when our troops were stationed there; the conditions of poverty and disease in developing nations to which we too often turned our backs; the pullout of troops and severing of diplomatic ties with Afghanistan after our government had used the country against the Russians, thus allowing the proliferation of terrorists and warlords; the threats against the Taliban for the sake of our own obsessive need for oil and natural gas; and the list goes on. It was becoming clear to me that the murder of my daughter was not an isolated event. Nor could it be explained by the simplistic and dichotomous view our then-president offered. I knew that I had to learn the truth about why Alicia was murdered, even though it would surely be a painstaking and arduous journey.

Consequently, I started reading, researching, talking, emailing, and attending briefings. I gathered information from the FBI and GAO (Government Accountability Office), lawyers investigating 9/11, government officials, NODA (National Organization for Disaster Alliance), government whistleblowers, September 11th family organizations, peace organizations, the Gore Commission Report, and the Congressional Findings Report. I wrote congressional representatives and the president, marched at protests, prayed, and tried to make sense of it all. It has been a disheartening journey, to say the least.

Chapter 17

The Dawning of a New Day

Days pass as dusk gives way to night and night unfolds into a brand new morning. With each new dawn comes a promise of joy, often unfulfilled, and of divergent roads from which to choose along our journey. Sometimes we stand at a crossroads, searching for a clue as to which way to go. In our minds' eyes, the choices look the same, yet knowing that the choice we make may affect our lives in ways not yet understood, we balk. Fear of the wrong choice leaves us frozen, unable to decide—or something deep within may give us a gentle nudge, urging us onward. Thus it is with life. We live fully within the grace of God, or we stand at the edge of life, longing for the courage and conviction to move ahead. In the meantime, another day is wasted or spent experiencing life peripherally, not fully immersed in its joy and our own regeneration.

A child of God awakens to the symphony of sounds and the majesty of the dawning day. The night was dreamily restful and peace abounds. She slowly stretches her rejuvenated body and breathes in the new life force that resounds with elation deep within her soul. Arising, she searches, longing for the rapturous beauty of dawn's first light, nature's first hue of gold. With unformed thoughts that words could not possibly convey about the utter magnificence unfolding before her, she is excited for the adventure that beckons her. The pure excitement of a glorious new day, full of promise, full of hope, full of joy, full of love—life itself—makes her yearn to engage in the promise that God's love is abundant and plentiful. Her eagerness to seize the day and embark on the new adventure that awaits is only tempered by her own self-imposed limitations and irrational fears. She easily sheds these with each cleansing breath. Life is too short and much too precious for her to be tentative. And each day fully lived brings her nearer to peace and harmony, to heavenly felicity, to the oneness of life, to God.

Let us each strive to live with such innocence and faith, peace and love. Let us do so from our free will founded in God's truth. As we come to the crossroads during our journeys, let us be in harmony with God's will as we venture forth with courage on the enlightened path; for, indeed, it will make all the difference. (Journal, November 1, 2001)

Grief is relentless and burdensome. Sometimes it feels like pulling a weighted sled that keeps getting heavier with each step forward. There is no escape from this overwhelming pain. I now have empathy for those who seek relief through medication, alcohol, drugs, or other excesses. Some days, you just feel completely overwhelmed. I knew that I had to confront these overpowering feelings face-to-face. I needed to feel them at the deepest level, look intensively at them, analyze them, process them, and work through them to get beyond them. After all, what was the alternative: depression, chemical dependency, numbing myself so that I couldn't feel, or just going nuts? This was the biggest challenge of my life. I have faced many difficult challenges before, but nothing like this. This was going to take every ounce of my strength, an abundance of love and compassion from many, and undying faith in God to sustain me.

There is another very important aspect of grief that we don't often acknowledge. I realized that my grief was also an honoring of the deep love I felt for my daughter. I owed it to her, my family, and myself to confront this confounding anomaly and find my way to the other side. I needed to get to a place of regeneration, a place where I could grow my love and compassion, a place where I understood truth in a purer form, and most importantly, a place where I could make a difference in the world.

Dear God, help us to be strong in our convictions, clear in our discernment of truth, righteous in our efforts to do good in the face of evil, and loving in all our actions. Gently guide us and soothe our weary hearts. Help us to let go of our egotistical will and allow Your divine will to guide our journey here on earth and beyond. Help us to love more fully, seek truth more avidly, and act forthrightly in accordance with these guiding principles. May Thy will be done on earth as it is in heaven. Amen. (Journal, October 14, 2001)

The journey through grief is an intensely personal struggle. It requires deep introspection, a willingness to look within. It requires that you do the painful work of sorting the confusing, agonizing thoughts and devastating feelings that haunt you day and night. Compassionate others help along the way, providing strength through their love and understanding. But when they are gone and the loneliness of the night pervades and encompasses, our strength of faith is truly tested. My faith is strong, built upon the pain of the past, the understanding that comes through intense soul searching, and a persistent quest for truth, love, and wisdom. It comes from the strength of an abiding love that connects me to God, as well as a deeper knowing that transcends human understanding. I am a part of God, as is all of life. God is within me. I intuit and feel this interconnection with God and all of life. At times, I sense that I am given a fleeting glimpse into the mystery, but only when I release my ego and open my heart. My faith and sense of knowing transcend other ways of seeing, hearing, or perceiving that define me as human. In its fullness, it is something not easily understood by conventional thinking. Yet this knowing strengthens my faith in the loving omnipresence and omniscience of God. It empowers me through times of struggle when the burden is heavy and my human will is weakened. My faith sustains me in my grief. For that I am eternally grateful.

Deep in the canyons of my soul,
I feel the distant echoes of my heart's longing;
I feel your essence;
I see your light shining forth;
I hear the gentle tones of your joyous laughter
somewhere in the distant hereafter.
You are in my heart,
in my mind,
within the depths of my soul.

My saddened heart yearns for your earthly presence,
but my mind serves as the harbinger
of the ill-fated truth
that you are gone.
Gone to the Great Beyond
where glory awaits,
where joyous laughter resonates,
where love reigns supreme,
where light shines forth in colorful radiance,
beaming truth to my understanding,
and acts of love manifest in accordance.

Journal, November 29, 2001

Chapter 18

Happiness Is...

Happiness is the manifestation of joy that is present within our soul. Joy comes from God's eternal love. As adults, we may not always feel this elusive joy. But children are naturally in a state of joy; their innocence and brightness of spirit are given abundantly as angels watch over them and fill them with divine love they play and frolic. Joy is God's love in action, His will for us. It fills our hearts and flows outward from us to share with others. True happiness comes from living in harmony with God's love. Alicia wrote of happiness in her journal at a time in her life when she was experiencing the pain of loss at the end of a relationship. Her words are profound and resonant, the result of personal wrestling. We have found great comfort in her writings as they reflect her internal thoughts about life, love, and her search for meaning. She wrote:

Happiness is such an elusive emotion. One day you're soaring on its wings, the next you're looking about hoping to catch a glimpse of its sunny magnificence, trying to convince yourself it was real and not just a memory of a fairy tale from childhood.

Over the years my recipe for happiness has changed: used to be, all I needed (or thought I needed) was a knight in shining armor. Then, it was a king and his kingdom; next, I just needed the kingdom—I could rule. What ingredients do I need today? An infinite amount of love to give and receive freely, a purpose, goal, destination; I'm still working on it.

Those who have known the greatest happiness have opened themselves to the most gut-wrenching sorrow. It's a gamble; you have to play to win. Or maybe those who have endured suffering have a greater respect for joy and can appreciate it wherever they find it: the smell of a rose, the sight of a baby, an old couple holding hands. And those who've lived their lives in a heart-numbing

cocoon of sanity, safety, and contentment don't have the capacity for pure joy.
(Alicia's journal, January 4, 1999)

Alicia knew what happiness was. She searched constantly for those
things that brought happiness to her and others. Throughout her
brief life she exuded joyousness as she went about her daily activities.
She could look around her in a world filled with strife and see peace;
everywhere she looked she saw love and goodness, because that was
what she was about. She could look into another's heart and connect
with their goodness, their God within. Her joy was infectious; her smile
reflected her deep love within; her heart was filled with compassion;
her lifelong quest was for understanding. She sought truth, and this
truth guided her acts of love as she went about her daily activities. She
was on an enlightened path.

Swedenborg proclaimed that through our uses in society, guided by
our love and understanding of the divine, we fulfill God's will for us.
By stepping outside of our selfish love and learning to give unconditionally to one another, we act in accordance with God's principles. God
is love. God is truth. "Truth is...like a garment; when not being worn,
it is merely pieces of material adapted for a body, but when it is put
on, it becomes clothing with a human inside". [6] Our divine path is to
love God with all our hearts and love our neighbor through our actions.
By acting in accordance with divine principles in all our human deeds
while utilizing our skills and gifts, we are performing our "uses." The
full effect of our uses has a power beyond our limited understanding, a
transformational power that aligns us with God's will for us.

Chapter 19

And Time Goes On

Autumn turned to winter, bearing the cold desolation that stirs the soul toward a longing for warmth, greater love, and the promise of new-found hope with the coming of spring. Our cold, stark "winter of our discontent" appeared to be heading toward a life of discontent as the sadness and pain lingered. As the lonely days of winter came to a close, I felt the weight of the world on my shoulders oppressing me, wearing me down, and distressing my soul. The coming of spring seemed fruit-less and empty. I did not want to go on. Life's daily routine had become a gruesome gauntlet. In my worst moments, I was standing at the preci-pice of a deep, dark chasm, about to spiral downward. I had to do some-thing to stop this searing pain in my heart, this sense of hopelessness that threatened to consume me. I prayed for clarity; I prayed for relief; I prayed for life to return to my broken heart. I prayed for my Alicia.

Several significant things happened during this time. During the winter of 2001–2002, Bev and I spoke out on issues of peace and justice, writing contentious articles about war and civilian casualties for news-papers and magazines and participating in documentaries dealing with the politics driving our country's military decisions. I felt a strong need to help others in seeking justice rather than exacting revenge. We abhorred the thought of further violence that would surely result in the killing of innocent people. I could feel God's power helping me to under-stand the "why" behind all of this violence, as well as the "what"—what to do as a country on the international stage to confront terrorism. From the first moments after Alicia's murder, even in the midst of the greatest pain one could ever imagine, I knew that I had to do my part to stop the cycle of violence. I knew that, in the end, these wars would only serve the forces of evil.

In this day and age the vast majority of war casualties are civilians, innocent civilians: children, the aged, parents, siblings, whole families. Justifying such atrocities aligns closely with the dark forces that killed our loved ones. Only love, a love that comes from God, can possibly overcome such evil. This does not mean we should ignore those who performed such acts of hatred and violence: justice must be served, but not through the killing of innocents.

Immediately after September 11, most of the world was behind the United States. The collective power of such support and the possibilities for collaboration were many. The time to join with other countries, to put aside petty differences and work toward a just world, was now. The time for the forces of good, based in principles of love and understanding common to all belief systems, to overcome these evil forces had come. But our country's response demonstrated the same mentality as that of the "evil-doers" who had perpetrated this assault against humanity. We waved our flags proudly as innocent Afghanis died alongside a few members of al Qaeda. Civilian casualties were many; the American public cheered the destruction of homes and whole villages; hatred for America escalated.

As war rages on and violence gives way to more violence, I feel the sad irony of the Christmas season's peace and joy. How many truly know the meaning of peace? How many have experienced the fullness of such joy? Peace is not merely the absence of war, nor a ceasefire in the midst of battle, nor perpetual readiness for war with the eerie silence of the guns and nuclear warheads aimed at strategic targets waiting for their launch. Peace goes much deeper. It is the feeling of God within and the faith that He will guide us toward harmony, love, and truth. Peace exists in the absence of hate, distrust, jealousy, anger, revenge, avarice, and fear. Peace comes from feeling our interconnectedness with all of God's creation and the harmony that results.

We are from God and God is within us. We are intricately interconnected in ways unfathomable by the human mind. We are like the cells that make up a body, each working in conjunction with the others for the optimal function of the whole. When cancer strikes, modern medicine wages war on the cancerous cells and attempts to kill them off with chemotherapy and radiation. In essence, we wage war on these cells in the hope that the good cells will regenerate and the bad ones will be eradicated. Someday we will discover that this extreme and violent way of approaching dis-ease is antiquated, disharmonious, and separate from the healing power of God. Waging war on our bodies to destroy bad cells—or waging war on one another because we haven't learned a better way of resolving conflict—seems so outdated, so primitive and desperate. This was the way of cultures throughout history who acted out of ignorance and fear, yet we continue to perpetuate this atrocity by narrow-mindedly reacting with fear and ignorance that doesn't take into account the underlying cause or the resultant effect. Dr. Martin Luther King Jr. summed it up best when he stated:

The ultimate weakness of violence is that it is a descending spiral, begetting the very thing it seeks to destroy. Instead of diminishing evil, it multiplies it... Through violence you may murder the hater, but you do not murder the hate. In fact, violence merely increases hate...Returning violence for violence multiplies violence, adding deeper darkness to a night already devoid of stars. Darkness cannot drive out hate; only love can do that.[7]

The tragic events of September 11th and the murder of my daughter will forever change my life. In many ways, it will change the world. There exists within each of us an opportunity to strive for greater understanding and deeper love. If we came together to raise human consciousness, to reach out to those in need, to embrace all peoples from around the world as our brothers and sisters, we could make a difference in ways that would ultimately lead to peace and harmony...to the joy of heaven here on earth. By our choices and our actions, we can make a difference.

May God be with us in this time of spiritual transformation. May we all feel the love of God within our hearts, experience the enlightenment of truth, and feel the true essence of peace and wondrous joy throughout this season celebrating the birth of the Christ Child on this earth and within each of us. Let there be peace on earth and goodwill toward all. (Journal, December 14, 2001)

After Christmas we received a call from a producer in Hollywood who wanted to create a documentary about 9/11 from a perspective that aligned with ours. We talked on several occasions and, although the documentary never materialized, she provided us with a connection with other September 11 families who were speaking out for peace and justice: September 11th Families for Peaceful Tomorrows[8]. This organization would prove our saving grace, helping us turn our grief into action for peace. And the beautiful people who had chosen peace over revenge would become significant in our grieving. We resonated with these incredible individuals who felt no need for vengeance and responded to the deaths of their loved ones on a higher level of understanding; they too felt the interconnectedness of all people.

Many families of the victims of September 11, 2001 were not of the same mind. But the 200 or so families and several thousand supporters who comprised the Peaceful Tomorrows group were unified in their desire to address the root causes of war and find peaceful alternatives. We wanted to uncover the truth behind the terrorists' attacks, our government's failure to prevent them, and the proactive steps we could take to avoid further attacks. We also wanted those responsible for the attacks of 9/11 brought to justice in an international court of law.

Initially, we communicated with our newfound friends from afar and coordinated our efforts for media responses, speaking engagements, and documentaries. The 9/11 families who lived in closer proximity joined together for organized activities. We now felt supported and affirmed in our purpose, and we felt very strongly that this was what we needed to do. Alicia would have wanted us to use our grief to propel us toward alternative solutions without further killing.

Today my soul is singing, but the melody is etched in sadness with only a tiny seedling of joy. Yesterday I could hear no song. The sun shone complacently on my desolate soul, and the song of life seemed so distant and faint. Today the raindrops cleanse my grieving heart and quench my thirst. I longingly searched for truth and sought strength for my weary legs. I was given a sign that spoke to my heart and beckoned me to take heed.

Merely happenstance, one might surmise. Yet, knowing how life answers heartfelt calls, I trudge onward, knowing that the answers to life's perplexing problems lie ahead of me. I feel reassured that life's mystery will become clear along the journey. I must choose wisely, lest I stumble and fall or find myself upon a path that leads somewhere other than my heart's desire, someplace where ego entices me onward with the illusion of happiness. I know that I must follow God's will on this path. I must heed God's call and boldly go forward with meaning and purpose, guided by my higher power.

Seek and ye shall find; ask and ye shall receive. (Journal, February 19, 2002)

Rays of illumination and hope find their way through the clouds of despair and depression. Just when you think you are at the end of your rope and the weight of the world is more than you can bear, love finds its way into your heart and a new path shines forth. I realized I needed to cherish these moments because they are too often short-lived and fleeting. Faith helps to sustain me.

I sit wondering at the mystery of God's creation as I gaze at the majesty before me. The dark silhouette of the evergreen-covered mountains graces the horizon of the pale blue sky; the morning sun shines its brilliant golden light on the snow-covered peaks of the surrounding mountains, creating sparkling diamonds amidst the pure white snow; cedar and aspen trees stand firm, like sentries protecting a queen; God's creatures scurry about to keep from freezing on this crisp Montana morn. An all-encompassing peace echoes from the stillness of nature's soul.

My soul longs desperately for the same sense of peace and harmony that graces life with the morning light and fills the brand new day with hope: that life will bestow blessings upon us this coming day, with the promise of sweet joy and abundant laughter; that all fears and anxieties from the day before will have righted themselves; that all the pain that so consumes the heart will dissipate and the void in my heart will be filled with the love that has been so tragically taken away.

Life is such a precarious balance. One day you're riding high on its wings as laughter flows freely from your soul. Your heart opens to the birds singing their sweet sounds; loved ones are savoring life and growing in spirit, as God has intended. Then tragedy strikes without warning, without provocation, and shatters your world; pain becomes your constant companion. For a moment, suspended in time, God seems to have let something slip by. Evil has reared its ugly head and all hell breaks loose. You ask, "What is the purpose of such devastation? Why, dear God, do you allow evil forces to destroy the lives of innocent people? What good can possibly come out of such hate and destruction?"

If only I could know the truth that my soul seems mysteriously to understand. Somewhere in the deep recesses of my soul's knowing, all of this makes some kind of sense, but my heart screams for justice and a righting of this terrible wrong that has taken my dear sweet Alicia from me. God rest her soul. (Journal, March 2, 2002)

The promise of springtime normally fills me with the anticipation of new energy, renewed hope, and abundant love; but not that spring. I searched deep within my soul for direction, for hope, for God. Lo and behold, the answer came. I realized what I needed to do.

As I went about my work routine (during the moments when my mind could stay focused on the tasks in front of me), I realized that I needed to make a life change. Herein lies the dilemma: during grief, it is usually smart not to make any life-changing decisions. Give things some time, talk ideas over, then, after objectively analyzing and weighing options, make a well-thought-out decision. I was desperate, but I didn't want to do something I would regret later.

I decided to seek counsel with the president of the college, Dr. Conway Jeffress, a cool-headed, deeply intelligent man whom I had admired from afar but didn't know personally. I told him my dilemma; I couldn't stay focused on the things I needed to do when it came to dealing with the newly hired staff and subsequent changes in the program I had initiated prior to September 11. Those projects needed my full attention, but I couldn't tolerate sitting in meetings listening to others expound on purported "matters of consequence" that seemed so trivial. I was deeply sad and longed to be with my family—anywhere other than work. I told him I didn't even know if I wanted to continue in my current job. Try as I might, I couldn't hold back the onslaught of tears. I didn't care what happened. I just wanted my life back. I just wanted my daughter.

Conway surprised me with his heartfelt and thoughtful response. He asked me what I wanted to do: change jobs, create a new job, take time off, or something else. I thought about it and realized I needed to take time off to heal, to be with my family, to spend time in nature, and to receive some counseling. With this decision made, I felt renewed hope.

I had worked at some sort of job since childhood; even during college I had worked fulltime to put myself through school. Thoughts of all the possibilities that life had to offer flooded my mind, and a newfound excitement surged through my veins. I felt a surge of energy. It was time to let the healing begin.

I worked for a couple more weeks until all the arrangements were made with Human Resources for me to take some extended "sick time." I discussed strategies with my supervisor and staff. I tied up loose ends as best I could. I started seeing a counselor. Being a counselor myself, I wanted to hear the perspective of someone I could trust, someone with whom I could feel comfortable doing the difficult work of healing. After all, if I was going to entrust my life to the hands of another at a time when I was most vulnerable, I had to believe in both the person and the process.

I had previously interviewed local mental health counselors and was aware, to an extent, of their basic styles and credentials. I selected George (not his real name) to help me in my healing. George used a number of techniques that I could relate to, including a visualization/energy technique and a technique called neurofeedback therapy. I started seeing George twice a week for a while. One session would include neurofeedback; the other would involve talk therapy. The neurofeedback helped me feel that I was empowering my brain to process the overload of emotions, easing me through the depression and allowing me to work through the grieving without numbing myself with drug therapy. Drug therapy is appropriate for some, but widely overused and abused by many. I needed to feel the depth of my emotions, look at them introspectively, do something with them, and hopefully gain some semblance of control over them.

I wasn't looking for a magic cure or an easy solution; there are none when it comes to grief and loss. But I felt that greater understanding and renewal could be had through therapy, if I could find my way through the pain. My whole life had been fraught with intense challenges, challenges that had the power to make me stronger or to destroy me. I had overcome them in the past, and now, with God's help and the love of friends and family, I would learn to cope. For my family's sake, I had to do this. I had to because this was what life had imposed upon me. I had no choice.

As the day approached for me to leave work, I started to allow myself to think of things I could do to help the healing process. I thought that a hands-on project, an activity in which I could lose myself in physical labor without having to deal with complex human interactions required by my job, would be ideal. Consequently, I started building a stone patio and deck on the rear of our house. I labored to excavate the site for a couple of weeks, found some beautiful flat rocks called "Pennsylvania

Turnstone Lilac," assembled a deck, and created a new living space. Next, through the generosity of a neighbor who built houses for a living, we subcontracted help to remodel our kitchen. These projects were therapeutic. When they ended, I needed another physical outlet, so I decided to train for the San Francisco Chronicle Marathon and run it in Alicia's honor—it was the marathon she would never be able to run in her home city.

I found myself wanting less and less to be around people. I felt estranged from those who went about their daily lives as if all was well. They seemed to be spending vast amounts of time and energy on inconsequential things, talking about nothing in particular of consequence, repeating their daily routines without meaningful thoughts or a real sense of purpose. I was out of step with life around me. I didn't judge "regular people," but I couldn't blend in with this scene, not when the nightmare within my head incessantly attacked my heart and left me distraught and desolate. Even running an errand in town was painful— all the pleasant little smiles, small talk about nothing in particular, and the hassle of the effort itself. The only time life made sense was when I was out in nature, alone or with Bev, with my children or grandson. I spent a lot of time sitting alongside the river by our house, running or walking in the woods around the lakes, or watching the sun rise and set as the birds serenaded me with their songs. I felt the presence of God in nature, and life made more sense without the confusion of human beings, who could rationalize the violent murder of other human beings and justify it in the name of God. In nature, I could witness peace and harmony—testimony to my God's existence.

In May of 2002, I decided to take a road trip with Alicia's dog, Pollo. Alicia had rescued Pollo from an animal shelter when he was a puppy. He had grown into a beautiful blend of Husky, Lab, and who knows what else. He maintained much of his Husky heritage with his exceptional strength and coat, but his color was that of a yellow Lab. Alicia had loved him, but, as often happens when kids leave home, we had inherited him when she moved to California. Pollo and I decided to go camping in the wilderness of Michigan's Upper Peninsula. We would take a week and circumvent the UP, camping along the way. Bev supported me in my need to get away; she knew it would help me heal.

The day came for me to head north. I packed my Toyota 4-Runner with all the camping gear I would need. The north woods beckoned me onward, and I was hopeful for healing and a renewal of life. I stopped by to see a friend who lived along the shore of Lake Huron; I visited the majestic Tahquamenon Falls; I camped along the scenic shores of Pictured Rocks along Lake Superior; I hiked along the shore of Copper Harbor; I backpacked and camped in the beautiful north woods and lakes of the Porcupine Mountains. It was all incredibly beautiful, filling

my soul with a sense of peace. But the pain in my heart left me bur-
dened and bowed down. I missed my daughter. And nothing could
repair the sadness in my heart.

Chapter 20

Day by Day

Each morning, during that first year after Alicia was killed, I would get up and write in my journal. Some days my entries came to me in a poem or prayer; other days, I just wrote whatever was on my mind. Tears would often stream down my cheeks as I wrote, but it was cathartic to process my inner thoughts and deepest fears, to attempt to put words to the myriad of overpowering emotions.

Having disconnected from the "rat race," the daily routine of work and all the customary activities that too often define who we are, I was able to look fully into the face of grief without distractions. The accepted grieving practice in our society—losing oneself in work to avoid feeling pain—had not worked for me. I would not use avoidance as a means to escape the inevitable, at least not to the degree some would choose. Sometimes diverting myself from the pain felt right, but I knew I eventually had to confront it. I knew with the utmost certainty that it was not going to go away by itself. My fractured world would not magically reshape itself into a new order if I did not confront it and strive to understand the phenomenon that had such a hold on my soul. By actively grieving and feeling the depth of my pain and sadness, I was healing and honoring the love for my daughter. She (and I) deserved nothing less.

There were moments along the way when seeds of hope would arise in the midst of the despair. One of those I tried to capture on my morning entry in May.

This morning's run felt like the runs from the past, prior to September 11. The sun was shining brightly; the temperature was fitting for a perfect spring day; the river shimmered like diamonds; joy was in the air. After the run, I spent time with my beautiful grandson, Logan, and it was wonderful. We drove around the yard on my John Deere tractor, and Logan helped steer. We decided to take a road trip in my little MGB and drove along the beautiful Huron River until we reached the Dairy Queen, then shared a chocolate ice cream cone. He was so very precious, sitting in the front seat with the top down, just taking it all in.

Upon our return, I listened to Sarah McLachlan and felt a wave of sadness as my mind tried to comprehend the full impact of the loss of my dear, sweet Alicia. It hurts deeply to think that I will never get to share these joyous moments with her, at least in this lifetime. Well-meaning people try to console me by saying, "You know you will see her again someday in the life beyond." And, I know this in the very depths of my being, but the sad reality is that I can't reach out and hold her in my arms; I can't laugh and reminisce with her like we once did; I won't be able to love and care for her children with that special grandpa's love; we can never dance again like we did when she was a child and later as an adult; and we will never be able to take the father-daughter trip to Alaska we had planned—or any other adventure. It's very little consolation for the sadness and pain in my heart to know that "someday, I'll see her again."

It has been a mystical and painful journey through grief thus far. The intriguing side of this arduous journey is that it bares the souls of those we come in contact with as they try to console us. Many compassionate and loving souls have come forth from unexpected places, while others from whom we had expected unconditional love and ongoing support seem to have put us on a shelf and retreated to their cozy little lives so they don't have to feel our pain and sorrow. In general, people don't know how to support those of us who are in pain and grief. Out of sight, out of mind. Don't get involved. Give them space; stay busy through work, and all will magically be made right.

I don't want their pity; I don't want their fake remorse; all I want is for good people to reach out to one another with love and compassion. After all, isn't that what life is all about? We can't live in isolation. What affects one affects us all in some way. When we are given opportunities to help a brother or sister in need, to do a good deed, or to reach out with love in the face of evil, we must step forward and act upon these righteous thoughts. When we do act on our heart's longings to do good, guided by the light of truth, we grow spiritually and the whole of humanity grows with us. What we do along our own journey should be in harmony with those around us, rather than a path of disharmony and self-serving desires.

After September 11th, people were given an opportunity to reach out to one another, to do good in the face of evil, and to grow collectively on our spiritual journey. Many people responded to this calling. Now, with the machinery of war in full force, many people seem to have retired into that protective cocoon of safety and sanity. "Hear no evil; see no evil" becomes their credo as they stick their heads in the sand, blindly accepting our government's actions without acknowledging or feeling the ramifications, without hearing the screams of the *dying children and their grieving parents. They fail to heed the pleas for help and the cries of anguish as our campaign of "shock and awe" devastates the lives and homes of the Afghani people. People retreat to their daily lives as the killing fields encompass the homes of innocent families, and we arrogantly act as if we are justified in our actions.* (Journal, May 2002)

The spring gave way to summer, normally a happy time of activity, travel, family, and friends. June was approaching, and I wasn't sure how I would handle one of the heretofore most joyous days of my life: the celebration of the birth of Alicia, my firstborn child. On June 11, 1973, Alicia came into this world and graced us with her presence. She was such a beautiful baby, our gift from God, conceived in love, who changed our world with her love and her deep sense of purpose. I sensed this from the onset. She was on a divinely inspired journey and would follow this course to the end. Her name means "truth"; her essence was love; her mission in life was to spread joy and instill peace in all whom she encountered. She is still doing all of this in the world beyond.

We decided to celebrate Alicia's birthday in Montana, at my son Zac and daughter-in-law Lana's lovely home near Helena. This newly built 7,500-square-foot bed and breakfast was designed and built by Zac's in-laws, Mark and Joyce. The fourteen-inch logs were shipped from Utah to build this magnificent structure surrounded by the Elkhorn Mountains. The spacious living room with its open stone fireplace gave way to a view of the mountains through four windows, each seven by nine feet. Eagles flew overhead and elk roamed the countryside. The silence of the outdoors was almost deafening as our ears searched for the usual commotion. We would gather together there and fill this day with Alicia's energy, joy, and fun. And we would feel deep sadness because she was missing.

We were joined by Greg; Alicia's good friends, Lyndsey and Tamara from San Francisco, Ray from Ohio; and my sister, Jodi, from Florida. Naturally, we headed up into the mountains to hike, camp, rock climb, and rappel. After we had parked the Land Cruiser and loaded up our gear, we started the ascent to the face of a huge cliff overlooking the lush valley below. We hiked and climbed until we came to the agreed-upon spot where we would set up camp. The location was vintage Alicia, with its formidable cliffs, majestic peaks, vantage points for scanning the countryside, and pure beauty all around. Now, if only the weather would cooperate!

It started raining, not just a gentle rain that we could easily negoti-ate, but a thunderstorm with its unpredictability and heavy rains. We huddled together under a tarp lean-to, beneath the overhang of the rock face that protected us on one side, and managed to get a fire going for warmth. We contemplated our next moves, but each of us knew that we would ride out the storm and hope for a better day tomorrow—symbolic of our own journeys in grief.

The winds finally subsided, the clouds dissipated, and the morning of June 11 brought sunshine and blue skies. It was a perfect day in many respects, which only served to amplify the feeling of emptiness at the absence of our birthday girl. Alicia's twenty-ninth birthday took place without her physical presence, but her spirit was fully alive and among us. We laughed as we drank our early-morning mimosas, a favorite of Alicia's, and we cried as we shared stories, Alicia stories that were uniquely hers. She always sparked such joy and laughter, and her vivaciousness was captivating. With each story we relished the richness of our memories, chased by the bitter aftertaste of our sadness. God, how we missed her! It just didn't seem fair.

Chapter 21

Running Alicia's Marathon

Training for a marathon is intense, even under normal conditions. It requires determination and strength that cannot wane. After building a base of thirty miles per week, the demands of the next sixteen weeks become progressively more challenging. Faced as I was with debilitating grief, I found myself training under conditions that were less than optimal. Quite honestly, that training proved one of the most difficult challenges of my life. But I had proclaimed that I was going to run the San Francisco Chronicle Marathon for Alicia. She had told friends that she was going to run a marathon one day. That day never came, so Shanoa, Greg, and I decided to run one for her. This was Alicia's marathon.

Alicia had always been in good physical shape. She loved spending time out in nature. We had often run, biked, canoed, mountain climbed, skied, and shared other adventures together. When she was younger, she would run the last few miles of the marathons with me in Boston, Columbus, and elsewhere, cheering me on and willing me to the finish.

Training for the upcoming marathon in the midst of grieving seemed impossible. I forced myself to trudge along even when my body resisted. I felt sluggish. I had no energy. My spirit was diminished. My heart ached and my will to go on waned, but somehow I trudged on. Finally the day came, but I was not adequately prepared and I knew it. Family and friends joined us in San Francisco in late July 2002 as we made ready for the grueling 26.2 mile trek through the city's hilly streets. The night before, I sat down and wrote in my journal:

Tomorrow morning at 6:00 a.m., 5,800 people will start en masse toward their goal of running 26.2 miles. For some, it will be their first attempt at such a feat. For others it will be a repeat performance. A few elite runners will blaze through the course at a five-minute-per-mile pace, while others will struggle to meet the imposed five-hour deadline, after which the course shuts down. The pain and sacrifice are incredible; the time and effort to prepare for such an endeavor are considerable; the reward is mostly intrinsic for the majority of participants. The elite are rewarded monetarily.

A marathon is something different for each person lining up on that long-anticipated morning. Their reasons for running vary: some run for health and well-being; some run to defy the aging process and its ever-tightening grip. A few run to prove something to themselves or others. Many run because they love running. Running is a gift. Children receive it in its intended form; they run because they can, much as baby birds fly when their wings are ready to carry them from the nest. Running races is also a social event. Runners are some of the most fun-loving people I know. Rarely does one meet runners who are moody, angry, depressed, or afraid of life.

Running is a reflection of how we approach life in general. In life we either settle for something less than our souls long for or need, or we pursue our dreams with passion and vigor. During the running of a marathon, I've often visualized my life as occurring along the same phases I am experiencing in the race. At the beginning, the excitement of the coming venture peaks. The adrenaline pumps through your veins as you feel the fullness of life propelling you onward. Initially it is hard to contain your enthusiasm; finding the optimal pace that will ensure a long and prosperous journey is difficult. Sometimes the energy is so intense that you surge ahead at a pace that will surely take its toll. Along the way, the enthusiasm dwindles as you realize the distance that lies ahead. Consequently, you re-evaluate and slow the pace down, realizing you are in this for the long haul. Life passes in front of your eyes as the miles tick off. Regrets and second thoughts enter your mind. Doubt begins to set in as your body starts to feel the painful effects of the vigorous, youthful pace you set at the start, which was much faster and more furious than it should have been. There are still "miles to go before you sleep" as you muster new will to overcome the pain and marshal the tired and aching muscles that have carried you along this journey. It's about stamina, opening up to the energy that abounds, refocusing and renewing the spirit in anticipation of the fruit of your labor at the end of the road: a reward for a journey fraught with the tears of labor and filled with a vision of hope. It becomes a search for meaning along the way as well. The joy is in the doing, in the giving back to the life that has been bestowed upon us. The finish line is only the beginning of a new journey further along the path.

So, tomorrow morning, Greg, Shanoa, and I will line up at the start of a new journey, the San Francisco Chronicle Marathon, to honor the life of our dear, sweet Alicia in the city she loved so dearly. Thoughts of Alicia will fill our minds, and her spirit will propel us onward. Hope for a better tomorrow will permeate our beings; a longing for peace will be in our prayers. Alicia was so full of life! Her enthusiasm was wonderfully contagious and abundantly given.

She lined up at the start of a sort of marathon every day of her life, anticipating a new day's journey that would lead her to another place, further along her path. At the end of the day she could look back at the miles she had trekked, assess the struggle it took to get where she now was, reminisce on the miles behind her, and give thanks for the life she had encountered along the way.

The joy and happiness we receive is reciprocal to the effort and struggle we expend along the journey. Perhaps those who retreat to their protective "cocoons of sanity, safety, and security" out of fear don't allow themselves to experience life's challenges. Perhaps they cannot feel the height of joy and the satisfaction of true happiness, as Alicia so astutely suggested in her journal. She lived each day with vigor and enthusiasm. She lit out on each new day's journey with a smile on her face and love in her heart. Life, for her, was an adventure to be experienced, a marathon of sorts; in order to reap the benefits, you must take the initiative and be fully engaged each moment along the way, each mile on the journey ahead. (Journal, July 27, 2002)

The Journey Begins

I arose at 4:45 a.m. after a fitful night's sleep. I could feel the surge of adrenaline and the anxious feeling of anticipation as the six o'clock hour approached. This was not a new experience for me; but it felt the same as the first time I had run a marathon. The difference was that I knew what to expect and, more significantly, I was doing this for my deceased daughter. I tried to center myself by breathing deeply, relaxing, stretching, and visualizing what I had to do. I knew that I was physically capable of finishing, but emotionally I felt less prepared. My pain had encumbered me with the weight of the world in my training and preparation. During each training run, my body would scream at me to stop. But somehow I persisted and never succumbed to the overwhelming desire to give up. At times, I continued on as tears stained my cheeks. I embraced the pain and the grief. After all, this was the marathon that Alicia would never have a chance to run. This was a proclamation that her soul lived on in the hearts of those who loved her so dearly. This was her city by the bay. The San Francisco Chronicle Marathon was going to be Alicia's marathon.

At 5:40 a.m., we made our way down the glass capsule elevators from the sixteenth floor of the Hyatt Regency at Embarcadero. The starting line was less than a block away. Other runners were milling around the hallways and making their way to the starting line. Several had the familiar look of someone about to go into battle, that look of, "What on earth have I gotten myself into?" The six o'clock hour was quickly approaching as we made our way to the designated starting place in front of the Ferry Building along the Embarcadero. The Oakland Bay

Bridge was but a short distance away and would serve as a reminder toward the end that the journey was near completion, God willing. We made our way to the crowded starting line, gave hugs and received words of support and encouragement from family and friends, and moved in among the throngs of people nervously awaiting the starting gun. There was an electrifying energy in the air as we made last-minute preparations to begin.

The gun sounded. I felt a burst of energy and, at the same moment, the pain of sadness in my heart. What was I doing? This wasn't going to bring Alicia back. But I was committed and in some small way, I knew this was what I needed to do, not only for my own healing but also to help others. This was the journey into the desert of my soul. This was the purging of the pain that threatened to break my heart in two. This was an opportunity to bring Alicia's spirit to life for all to see. This was a way to work through the debilitating grief that had such a grip on me. This was free will and life-force energy put to use; this was God manifesting through me. I was here of my own choosing. The training had forced me to maintain a healthy state of mind and wellbeing. I was in great physical shape, I had been eating for health and running efficiency, and I had a goal that kept me looking forward rather than sinking into the deep abyss that longed to pull me down. Grief is an alluring state of being that can render one helpless and hopeless. I needed something positive to focus my energy on, something that I could put my heart and soul into, something that would proclaim Alicia's vibrant spirit through expression.

I remember the day, back in October of 2001, when Greg and I were hiking and running along the mountainous terrain beside the Golden Gate Bridge and I had decided to run the San Francisco Marathon for Alicia. Greg, who had never run a marathon, responded swiftly without thinking it through: "I'll run it with you." I was elated that he would commit to such a test of endurance. I was even more thrilled when Shanoa proclaimed that she would run it with us. The triad was complete, but the long, hard journey lay ahead, and we had many miles to go.

The stage was set and the curtain was drawn, but the actors had only begun the play. Many hours of preparation and numerous miles lay ahead of us as we began our own Trail of Tears. Eight months of tearful training runs and more than a thousand miles later, the healing run had begun. My legs and my body had given me many messages along the way that this was not going to be easy. But I knew that Alicia was going to be right beside me, as she had been in my previous twelve marathons, cheering me on and giving me strength. And indeed she was.

I ran in a state of reverence as we moved along the course together. Like a giant centipede, the runners moved as one, each controlled by a separate brain and motivated by diverse and varied reasons, but propelled toward a common goal. The panorama unfolded as the miles clicked along. The hills were merely hurdles that had to be mastered, but they added some unique changes to the otherwise scenic but cumbersome route. The Embarcadero gave way to Fisherman's Wharf, which led into bike paths along the bay. The long hill leading us around the structural art-form building near the Golden Gate Bridge was followed by the run through the Presidio. The headwinds along the North Beach were refreshing, but challenging nonetheless.

At the halfway mark, a gun went off as I was heading downwind along the same route along the shoreline. Hundreds of fresh-legged runners came barreling along on the much shorter half-marathon. I was feeling confident, despite some minor leg pain, when all of a sudden I felt a sharp pain in my left knee that threatened to stop my progress. I stopped and massaged it with some arnica cream I had had the foresight to carry with me. I was resolved to finish what I had started, even if I had to hop to the finish line on one leg. Thankfully, the intense pain diminished to the point that I could run on it.

I continued on my journey and made my way toward Golden Gate Park with all of its landscaped beauty and intense hills, which now seemed endless. I was approaching the 19.5-mile point when I could feel my energy depleting and my emotions sinking into despair. I prayed fervently: Dear God, give me strength to carry on. I had made a pact with Alicia prior to running this race: I would do the first 20 miles if she would help me with the final 6.2 miles, as she had done in the past.

Just as I was starting to sink into a marathon funk, shuffling lifelessly along to the finish line as I had done in my previous marathon at Big Sur after my father-in-law's funeral, a miracle happened. All of a sudden someone said, "C'mon, let's do this for Alicia." I looked up and saw a young man, Rajeev, holding out his hand and smiling. I grasped his hand for a few seconds and felt a surge of energy as we picked up the pace to its previous level. I looked up and saw Alicia's smiling face hovering above me, urging me on. Rajeev and I talked at length, and I told him about Alicia. He was empathic and inspirational as I glided along the next six miles at a faster pace than I had run the previous twenty miles. I had been given an inexplicable boost. Alicia had stayed with me to the finish, her sparkling eyes urging me on, just as she had done during my other marathons. Her spirit smiled down upon me at the finish line, confirming her presence even in death.

When I crossed the finish line, the physical and emotional effort of running for three hours and twenty-seven minutes hit me like a ton of bricks. I exploded with the pain of the deep, suppressed sadness as the waves of grief slammed me down once again. My emotional response was intense but, thankfully, shortlived as I lumbered to the recovery area and made my way to my room to recharge before returning to cheer Greg and Shanoa on to the finish line. We all made it, thanks to hard work and Alicia's energizing spirit. As I cheered my courageous, loving Shanoa to the finish line, I felt another surge of energy.

Alicia is still with us—that is clear. But life is forever changed, and the journey to accepting this new reality is long and arduous.

Running a marathon is probably not typical grieving behavior, but we have to do whatever we can to cope. Alicia loved this city. This was her marathon. And indeed, she was with each of us as we ran. (Journal, July 28, 2002)

Reflections

Sometimes I wonder what this life is about. I wonder whether this journey is our only time in human form, or if we might return. After all, our souls are energy. We are a part of the Source of all energy; we are a part of God.

I also ponder the mystery of life and why some of us are born into a life of pain and struggle while others have smooth sailing along the way—or so it appears. Is it that our souls, together with God, choose a path of greater resistance to help us evolve both individually and collectively? All we have to do is look at history and find examples that stand out so clearly: Jesus, Dr. Martin Luther King, Jr., Gandhi, Helen Keller…Their struggle and sacrifice led to greater good; their examples, their wisdom, and indeed their love for all of humankind made this world better for generations to come. But the many changes we must endure are sometimes overwhelming and fraught with pain.

Change is the only constant in this perplexing world. Those who resist this reality find themselves at odds with life itself, while those who accept this often painful reality can make the adjustments necessary when they find themselves victimized by life. I have always embraced change and looked forward to the resulting regeneration of my soul: I love the changing of the seasons, with all of their magnificence and grandeur; the changes that occur as we mature and go through our processes of development; the changes that help us grow our love and understanding; and the many transformations that unfold before our very eyes in daily life. Life is full of change. But not all of these changes are predictable or pleasant. Changes resulting from the death of a loved one are extremely painful. They seem to threaten our very perception of what is right and good. They attack our belief systems, challenge our values and morals, and force us to come to a new understanding of life and death. Change is inevitable. Death is inevitable.

I'm approaching the first anniversary of Alicia's death. Sometimes it hurts with the same ache as it did in those first months. Sometimes I find myself wondering if I'll ever be able to move on or feel joy as fully as before. It's hard to let go of someone you love so deeply. The love of a parent for a child connects one with the other. It feels as if this child of my loins is an extension of my own soul. There is no greater love. This is what God intended for us: to feel that depth of love, to feel joy in another's joy, to feel pain in another's pain, and to want everything good with all your heart and soul for your children. I cannot even imagine my life without my children, even at the risk of losing them. They have shown me truth and love, they have brought meaning to my life, they have given me a reason for living that sustains me, and they have instilled a joy in my life greater than any other joy.

So how does one cope with the violent death of someone so intimately connected and deeply rooted to his own soul? How does a parent come to grips with the ruthless murder of his child? How can one possibly move beyond such a tragedy? How will I ever learn to cope?

We've often heard it said that God never gives us more than we can handle. That's not entirely true. I don't think my friends Ben or Kevin or the many others in this world who've committed suicide understood this concept. Or perhaps they didn't feel that connection with God that gives us the strength of knowing and the faith to endure. Certainly there have been times when life seems overwhelming and hope is but a word bereft of meaning. I have been there many times in the past year, but always there has been something that keeps me going: family, friends, kind words, or someone reaching out their hand with compassion and love...God made manifest. (Journal, August 8, 2002)

Chapter 22

The Joy of Travel and the Mire of Politics

Bev and I had always wanted to travel and see the world. Italy was one of the places we longed to see. We had said we would go there for our twenty-fifth wedding anniversary, but instead we renewed our vows in the Thousand Islands of Ontario near Gananoque, our family vacation spot. Now, even though we were in the throes of grief, with gnawing depression threatening to consume us, we knew we had to do something exciting and adventurous. Even if we were only going through the motions of living life, we needed to pursue the things for which our souls had once desperately longed. Consequently, we started planning our trek through Italy. Lois, a dear friend of my sister, worked as a travel agent and offered to help us make the arrangements. We gave her an idea of where we wanted to go and the type of experience we were hoping for, and she checked out the options and made the arrangements. She was such a blessing in our planning, and the trip would prove a godsend in our healing.

In late August of 2002, we boarded the jet in Detroit, heading to Venice by way of New York City. We flew on a Boeing 767, the same kind of plane Alicia had died in as it exploded into the South Tower. I found myself visualizing the drama that must have unfolded on her plane and where she would have been. I could see in my mind the terrorists in their strategic locations in First Class and Business Class. I could imagine where the flight attendants were as the hijacking began. I could even visualize the stabbing of the flight attendant and the passenger as the terrorists maced the First Class Cabin in a diabolical plan designed to instill mass panic and confusion. Even though my mind had visualized Alicia in the back of the plane holding a small child, caressing his head and alleviating his fears, doubt lingered. It had not been confirmed where her station on the plane was; we would not know this for sure until much later, at an FBI briefing for the families. I could almost feel the fear, the panic, the desperation and fading hope as the plane made its way erratically toward New York City and its final destination—the South Tower of the World Trade Center. I found myself looking into the eyes of each person aboard our plane and planning a counter attack in case something happened.

Americans were no longer so complacent, nor would they be so accepting of the outdated training guidelines that the airlines had adhered to prior to September 11. Alicia had been given an emergency "special" training session just prior to her death on how to deal with a conventional hijacking. The problem was, even with the mounting intelligence about the pending hijackings that the airlines were vulnerable to, the authorities still focused their training on the outdated methods of the past: on how to maintain calm through compliance and cooperation, the assumption being that professionally trained teams would deal with the hijackers once the plane had landed. Ironically, there was mounting evidence that in future hijackings the planes would never land—and the airlines knew it according to FAA memorandums.

Maintaining their façade that everything was normal, the airlines went about business as usual, even though they had received 64 distinct messages from the FAA in the three months prior to September 11 offering strong evidence that the hijackers were planning to use the commercial jets as missiles and crash them into iconic targets such as the Pentagon, the White House, and the World Trade Center. The airlines refused to pass this information along to the flight crews, the airports, airport security, or the public, all because of the fear of losing business. The almighty dollar would dictate decisions allowing the tragedy of September 11 to unfold as bin Laden and his followers had planned.

The ineptitude of our government agencies, at all levels, in preventing what many knowledgeable people believed was quite preventable allowed the plot to unfold as planned. Large numbers of people around the world and in the United States believe that our government was complicit or even behind the 9/11 attacks. If "complicit" implies that they failed to act on critical information that clearly outlined the pending attack and did nothing in response to prevent it from happening, I would concur. The deliberate concealment of information for "national security reasons," the deceptive practices employed by President Bush, Dick Cheney, Condoleezza Rice, Donald Rumsfeld, John Ashcroft, Colin Powell, and other members of the Bush administration in building a case for war, only added to our grief. One thing of which I am absolutely certain, given all the facts that have emerged since the attacks, is that the horrendous tragedy of September 11, 2001 could have and should have been prevented. Meanwhile, the American public continues to stick its collective head in the sand while relying on pompous naysayers, extremist right-wing television and radio commentators, and local news teams for truth. I can say assuredly that truth won't be found there.

We arrived in Venice after a redeye flight and very little sleep. We found our way to the water taxi that would take us to the San Marco Piazza and our hotel. It was all surreal. As if life itself weren't complex enough, we found ourselves in a foreign country, in a city with canals for streets and architecture from a completely different time period— and we were deep in the throes of grief. But the beauty and wonder of it all was captivating, and at some level, my soul was elatedly anticipating the coming adventure.

Our hotel room was just off of the Piazza. We settled in and took a short nap, then wandered around in amazement, taking in the sites and scenes that unfolded before us. It was all like a dream; the ancient cathedrals, the historic buildings, the people, the outdoor cafes, the canals, the bridges, the gondolas, the narrow walkways between the buildings...and our minds were already filled with faraway thoughts of a loved one lost. But we were determined to make the most of our rekindled dream, our long awaited trip to Italy. We would later discover that it was a trip almost identical to one Alicia had planned out for herself before her death.

Italy: Her Soul Is With Us

Strolling along the narrow, carless streets of Venice this morning, well before the masses of tourists awakened, I was inspired by the romance of the architectural design, the numerous canals, and the Greek and Roman influence that is so prevalent. Surely in its original design and intent the creative genius here was inspired by the Divine. Art, music, and the elaborate designs everywhere create the aura of a surreal and glorious existence here on Earth that surely corresponds to the beauty of heavenly communities in their purest forms. Imagine the magnificence and the beauty of the world in its most perfect form! I believe this city gives us a fleeting glimpse of the ravishing loveliness that awaits us on the other side of life.

Tonight we will ride the gondola through the narrow canals that weave through this beautiful city. When we return, the sounds of Vivaldi will grace our ears with a resonant sweetness that fills the mind with thoughts of grandeur and soothes the soul with its heavenly tones. Through all of this wonderment, which is jaded by my grieving heart, I feel the comforting presence of our dear, sweet Alicia. I lightheartedly proclaim that she is our tour guide, as we seem to be guided to wonderful restaurants with angelic décor, to a magnificent concert hall that just happens to be performing one of Alicia's favorites, Vivaldi's Four

Seasons, and Pachelbel's Canon, which was the piece Bev and I chose as part of our renewal service four years ago.(Journal-August 2002)

Upon my return to the Hotel Ambassador Tre Rose, I sat down for breakfast and overheard a couple with a distinctive American accent. When the wife walked by, I asked her where they were from. She told me they were from Harlem in New York City; her name was Gwen. As we talked, I told her about Alicia. She offered her condolences and returned to her table.   Not long afterward, her husband, Walter, came over and sat down beside me. He had helped with the cleanup of the World Trade Center site. He told me that he was very upset about the way things had happened because a week prior to September 11 he had received information that indicated the date of the attack. At the time he hadn't realized the tragedy that was about to unfold. He was riding in a cab in New York City and was talking to the African-born cab driver, who was Muslim. They were chatting about their travels. He indicated to the cab driver that he would be traveling on September 11 to a common destination that they had been discussing. The cab driver very matter-of-factly stated that the airports would be shut down that day and he should change his plans. Walter didn't think much about it until afterwards, when the impact of the cabby's statement hit him like the collapse of the towers. During the clean-up work at the WTC Site, Walter talked with many of the policemen, firemen, and volunteers helping there. The general consensus among the workers was that the FBI had known the attack was going to occur, but neglected to act on the information. There is mounting evidence that confirms this perception.

I believe in the United States of America, but I feel strongly that someone dropped the ball on this one. Our government agencies sat on vital information that could have prevented this tragedy from occurring. Idealist that I am, I hope that the truth will be made known and that a more concerted and cooperative effort will be made to prevent such tragedies from happening again. More effort must be placed on developing proactive conflict resolution strategies before they escalate to catastrophic levels. We *are* our "brother's keepers." All human beings are a part of a single family called humanity. It's far more self-serving and convenient to isolate, alienate, and hate than to assume some responsibility for the world's hungry, poor, sick, and needy. If America is to be a true leader, inspired by God's righteousness, we must expand our thinking beyond our own selfish and political interests. I know that there are no racial barriers in heaven—and I know in my soul that hate and violence do not dictate policy there. I also know that we have a long way to go even to come close to having a heavenly community here on earth, but we must start somewhere, or we will surely destroy each other.

I have experienced the intense pain of losing my daughter to hatred and violence. My heart goes out to those people in the world who have felt this kind of loss. Why do we humans keep doing this to ourselves? It's not as simple as some would have us believe. It's not so dichotomous as good versus evil, or right versus wrong. After all, I wonder how the Afghani civilians who have lost a loved one to our misguided missiles and tactical mistakes are feeling about the benevolent efforts of the United States. War and the killing of innocent people is not the pathway to peace. During the twentieth century, according to Robert McNamara in his book *Wilson's Ghost*[9], 160 million people died as a result of war. Seventy-five percent of those people, according to estimates, were civilians. When will we stop this human carnage?

The Ugly Face of Politics

Losing someone we love, especially a child, is perhaps the worst pain we will face on this earth. Throughout my life, I have been truly blessed, the greatest blessing being my family, for which I am ever so thankful. I have also felt the searing pain of loss: of my beautiful fifteen-year-old nephew, Gabriel; of several close friends; of a sister-in-law; of grandparents with whom I was very close; of aunts and uncles who had taken on the role of surrogate parents; of an eleven-month-old nephew, Titus; of my father-in-law and others. I have also had several surgeries, motorcycle wrecks, car-bicycle collisions, and a number of other "painful" experiences, all of which were extremely taxing. I thought I could handle pain and loss. I thought that my constitution was strong and my connection with God was deep enough to handle most anything. But I was not prepared for the violent murder of my firstborn child. I don't know that we can ever be prepared for something as soul-wrenching as that.

To complicate my grieving, I began to see quite clearly that politics were deeply involved in the September 11 attacks on the United States. I researched extensively, read avidly, and talked with others who had keen insight into the politics of 9/11. I witnessed the cover-up of vital material for political reasons at the 9/11 Commission hearings. Our lawyers spent millions of dollars and many hours of investigation uncovering the truth about why and how the terrorists were funded, only to be thwarted by our own government in the process. This harsh reality was more than Bev and I could bear. All we wanted was the truth about why our daughter was murdered. All we wanted was honesty, transparency, ownership of responsibility, and the whole ugly truth of why and how.

As I said before, I believe in our country. Our founding fathers and the American ideal have brought us to a place of world leadership and respect. The common people of the United States are good, honest, and hardworking. But the fact that our government failed us miserably, both before and after the September 11 tragedy, is deeply painful and utterly distressing. Knowing that my country's policies and politics could have prevented this heinous crime has been disheartening, to say the least.

The tragedy of September 11, 2001 could have been prevented. I say this with a deep conviction that comes from exhaustive research and intensive investigation—from reading tens of thousands of pages of analyses by journalists, politicians, intelligence personnel, government whistle blowers, former terrorists, lawyers, and from conversations with many of these people. That conversation with Walter in Venice opened my eyes to my need to start looking for answers, for truth. For Alicia's sake, for the sakes of the other three thousand men and women whose lives were taken on that September morn, and for the sake of my own healing, I had to know.

This is the quagmire in which I have found myself wallowing after Alicia became an innocent victim, a political casualty. Politics is ugly, with its hidden agendas, national security "secrets," and convoluted decisions that need to be made on a daily basis. Politicians have their own interests and personal agendas, which are often completely self-serving. In a democracy, the people have a right and an obligation to hold our elected officials accountable. This accountability includes honesty and transparency about their failure to protect citizens and their reasons for waging war.

Back to Italy

Our journey through Italy was a dream come true in the midst of our worst nightmare. The contrast was overwhelming, but Alicia was with us every step of the way. Looking back, I have the distinct sense that it was all a dream: the trip itself, all the wonderful experiences, the magnificence of the country...except for Alicia's presence, as she graced us with her essence to help us heal and lead us to inner peace. My journal tells the story.

Roma

Rome is in many ways another big city, very cosmopolitan, densely populated and culturally diverse. The Ambassador Hotel is not far from the train station and the surrounding neighborhood has a distinct Indian and Asian influence. Like many major cities, noise and air pollution are all around, even though the vehicles are economically designed—some electric, many motor scooters, and all very small in size. The air is filled with the smell of exhaust, and people zip around like bees that have been stirred from their nest.

The beauty of the city lies in the striking contrast between old and new. The ancient ruins intertwine with the modern structures and weave their way through the heart of the city. The distinct feeling that history is coming to life suggests a movie in which time travel has taken us back to the Roman Empire in all its glory. Especially poignant for me are the reminders of my namesake, Emperor Titus, even though his reign was a dark moment in the history of mankind. The Coliseum, finished by Titus in 80 AD, and the Arch of Titus still stand proudly for all to see.

When I think of the Roman Empire, the reminders of human greed and power and the atrocities that resulted deeply sadden me. These historical moments should remind us all in modern-day America of the darker side of humanity, but the lessons seem to escape us. God is within each of us. We are blessed with unknown potential to achieve wondrous things. The process of human spiritual evolution is a gradual movement toward spiritual enlighten-ment, the return to God, but progress is slow. History repeats itself again and again, but the sage lessons of loving our neighbor, having compassion for those who are suffering, and holding out hope for a joyous existence for all seem to elude us. Like our Roman forefathers, we wield power and wealth like a sword. We demand blind allegiance from those under our rule. We build awesome and majestic structures that proclaim our power in the world. And we develop weapons of mass destruction and war machinery, striking fear in the hearts of those who dare to stand against us. The chasm between the ruling class and the peasants, the haves and have-nots, is ever widening. We perpetuate jealousy and hatred through our arrogant attitudes toward those unfortunates who do not belong to the elite ruling class.

For most people, life has returned to "normal" since the strike on the World Trade Centers and the Pentagon last September. For some of us, the loss of a loved one will forever serve as a painful reminder that our world is in dire need of further spiritual growth and healing. The perpetrators of this atrocity against mankind will not be swayed from their twisted thinking and evil ways. They have chosen a course that aligns itself with hate, destruction, and evil. But the grassroots followers who blindly search for something to believe in and someone to lead them from their devastated lives and pain-filled existences—these are the ones who might respond to human compassion and brotherly love, if only it were offered.

As America and the world respond to the violence of that horrific September morning, we will determine the kind of world our children and grandchildren are to inherit. Violence and hate fueled these acts against us, and what has our response been? We react with more violence and hate, and hide behind the self-righteous veil of justice. We saw this coming. But what did we do to prevent it? How have our policies continued to fuel the flames of hatred? Why did we let those responsible for initiating these acts of terrorism run free when it was clear that they would strike America as they had done before? Why did we supply arms and training to these very people when it served our own purposes, knowing full well the hatred they harbored for America? How have we sought to change and help those youth who blindly followed and took up arms against us?

Violence follows violence. Hate only fuels the flames of passion for more hate. We look to our political leaders to show us the way through this time of confusion, anger, and fear. They responded with more of the same. In their eyes, the only way to react to violence is with retribution and a highly advanced war machinery. In the early days of human culture, it was bigger clubs and sharper sticks. Peace, in the eyes of our leaders, is merely the absence of war. But peace is much deeper and more profound than this simplistic overview suggests. Peace is a spiritual state that recognizes the presence of God, a feeling of at-one-ment in which we exist in harmony with all of life.

I believe that we are from God. We can return to God of our own volition through the choices we make and the direction we take in life. Some of us choose a path that leads away from God, yet the grace of God is forever with us. My actions are sometimes counter to my concept of God, but I strive to develop my understanding of divine truth and divine love and to manifest these through my daily actions.

When I search for evidence that we, as a human race, are evolving spiritually and striving to return to God, from whence we came, I find confirmation. Yet at the same time, I see us making the same mistakes over and over again, reacting out of fear, abusing our power, and acting from greed. We still have much work to do.

My daughter was violently murdered by hate-filled men who struck at the heart of America. But they also struck my heart and the hearts of the other loved ones of those murdered. Innocent Afghani children have been killed by our attempts to rectify the wrong done to us. How do those grieving parents and loved ones view the United States? After the bombs stop, with their country in shambles and their children dead, what perceptions and conclusions will they come to about the United States of America? What will they instill in the minds of the generations to come about right and wrong? About love and hate? About truth and justice? About power and greed? About the United States? When will the violence and hatred ever cease? (Journal, August 25, 2002)

Villa Vannini-Toscana

Throughout our travels across Italy in celebration of our upcoming thirtieth wedding anniversary, Alicia continued to bless us with her presence to help us work through our grief. Although the memories comforted our grieving spirits, the cavernous void felt painfully deep and overwhelmingly vast.

We tend to create our reality through our earthly perceptions while losing sight of the spiritual reality. Now we must open ourselves further to the deeper reality and experience her joyousness in ways that are different than before.

Our children bring deeper meaning and renewed purpose to our existence here on Earth—and new hope for a better tomorrow, a peaceful tomorrow. I hope that my children will not have to experience the depth of pain that I've had to endure. I hope for them all the joy that life has to offer, a protective love that will surround their hearts, and the light of truth that they may always see clearly.

But I know that they have their own divine purposes to fulfill. Alicia's spiritual course on this earth was more profound and painfully tragic than many. She came to us with a very distinct purpose: to make a difference in this ailing world of ours. I sensed that from the very beginning of her short life. I knew that she was special, and that she was going to have an impact in a big way. She seemed to have a more nuanced sense of what life is all about; she seemed to have greater depth and an immense reservoir of truth and love. Her soul had evolved in the light of God, becoming capable of tremendous love and compassion. Alicia was all of that and much more. Her evolved soul could absorb the hate and violence that took her life; her spiritual presence was needed on that inauspicious day in September to help others through the turmoil and confusion. Alicia was a beacon of light and a breath of fresh air in the midst of darkness and death.

It has been nearly a year since her soul moved on. I believe where she is to be heaven, yet, with all of the conjured misconceptions and limitations placed on this concept by many religions, I prefer to think about it more expansively. Emanuel Swedenborg explains heaven as being composed of different levels or societies, distinguished by the levels of truth and love put to use that their inhabitants have achieved in life. He states, "The angels of one heaven are not all together in one place, but are distinguished into societies, larger and smaller, according to the differences of the good of love and faith in which they are. Those who are in similar good form one society."[10]

Upon dying, we find our way to the spiritual community that matches our own soul's development. I know that Alicia is in a beautiful, loving, innocent, peaceful, learned heavenly society, and continues to grow and do God's work for good and truth. She is in the company of God's angels who have evolved equally in the light of truth and love. I feel her sense of peace and joy in her new existence. I feel her peace and see her angelic glow when she graces me with her presence.

One year has come and gone. It seems so fleeting at times, yet in some ways it feels much longer. When I try to imagine how it felt to hold her in my arms and to gaze into her joyous, loving eyes, it feels like a lifetime ago. Yet I can feel her essence in times of need, as she comes to me to console and bring healing love. I know with all the depth of my knowing that she is still alive on the other side of life. My earthly being longs for her physical presence, but my soul feels the peaceful resonance of her soul.

On our last night in Firenze (Florence), we walked through the city; gazed upon the river from the Piazza della Signoria, filled with statues and architectural masterpieces; ate across the river at Bibo's Ristorante; and leisurely walked back through the city as the evening fell. We stopped in the Piazza to watch the people and listen to a band that was playing in front of a restaurant. Both Bev and I were feeling a nostalgic sadness, which is how the pain of our loss often manifests. The wine-glow softened the edge somewhat, but could never mask the immensity of our feelings. Yet we could feel the magnificence and wonder of God's creation in this beautiful Italian city. We were sitting on the concrete base of a lamppost in the middle of the Piazza, and I could clearly feel Alicia's presence there with us. Bev was noticeably sad; tears fell on her cheeks.

At that very moment, a little girl of about two years old, walking with her mother, grandmother, and baby brother in a stroller, stopped and came our way. She fixed her sparkling brown eyes on Bev. Clearly, they were just passing through on their way to somewhere else, but this angelic little girl boldly walked over to us and refused to budge when her mother and grandmother urged her onward. She was determined to sit down beside Bev and me, the whole time gazing into Bev's eyes with a look of pure innocence and love. She wore a little sundress and sandals, just like the kind Bev had dressed Alicia in when she was that age. I could sense that she felt our pain; her eyes looked beyond our exteriors into our souls. She emitted peace and healing as she sat there gazing up at us. Her mother and grandmother tried to coax her to come with them, but she refused to leave. At the same time, the band started playing "September Morn." Needless to say, the tears streamed down our cheeks, but Alicia's presence was evident in the eyes of that little angel-child who was sent to comfort us. God surely works in wondrous ways.

Our last day in Florence was hectic. I had leased a car from a lot about ten minutes away from the hotel in which we were staying. Even though the agency was only ten minutes away (or so I thought), it became quite apparent that "you can't get there from here." I kept finding myself on one-way streets that took me somewhere I didn't want to be. My concentric circles got larger and larger as I tried to make my way back to the Hotel. The traffic was insane even by U.S. standards. What appeared to be one lane of traffic became three lanes, with motor scooters buzzing on both sides and in between the cars. The intersection circles reminded me of New Jersey, but with more exits and entrances. I felt like Chevy Chase in the movie European Vacation.

Consequently, the trip back to the hotel took about an hour and a half. By then Bev had already checked out and our bags were piled up in the lobby. My first experience of driving in an Italian city was followed by a trek into the mountains of the Tuscany region. Our directions were sketchy at best, but we knew the direction in which we were supposed to be going. When we stopped in one of the villages along the way to ask directions, all we got was a lot of hand gesturing and a barrage of Italian, some of which we could make out an occasional word. Finally, after driving up into the mountains on narrow, twisting, turning roads and getting lost (or "misdirected," as I choose to call it), we found our way to the road leading us to the Villa Vannini, the lovely inn where we were to stay.

The trip up the mountain was not without adventure, however, as the road was only wide enough for one small car and riddled with switchback turns that sent you back 180 degrees, with cars coming down the mountain toward you. But the charm and grace of the Villa Vannini, built in 1780 as a summer residence for the nobles of Pistoia and Firenze, made it all worthwhile. It had all the coziness of a bed and breakfast with the elegance of a fine hotel. Marta and Luigi, a married couple who were perfectly suited to their chosen profession, managed the inn. Luigi, the chef, spent hours making Tuscan meals. Marta was the perfect hostess, full of warmth and charisma as she provided for our comfort.

During dinner the first evening, which we enjoyed along with three other couples from various spots in Europe, Italian music was playing in the background. Bev and I began to unwind from the somewhat hectic day with a glass of Toscana wine and a five-course meal that would take two and a half hours to finish. Eating is an event in Italy, much more so than in the U.S.

Somewhere along the culinary journey, we began to feel Alicia's presence; the music suddenly shifted to songs that had special meaning to us. A series of about six or seven songs played that we had used in Alicia's memorial service or that were favorites of hers. Was this string of intensely meaningful songs merely coincidental? I don't believe that for an instant. Alicia was letting us know that she is alive and well, only in a different capacity. Our trip to Italy was the type of setting and adventure that Alicia loved. She was confirming her presence and helping us heal.

It doesn't take scientific proof to assure me that these incidences are indeed real. All it takes is faith in a wise and loving higher power, a mystical presence that is beyond our ego-controlled thinking mind, the source of unexplained phenomena and miracles. I feel a tinge of sorrow for those who do not recognize the presence of God. Life would be so limiting if everything were confined to our five senses! Faith comes from an understanding that truth transcends mere intellect and the constraining walls of the ego. The ego protects its self-serving boundaries like a sentinel standing guard over a vast, barren desert. The ego blocks the influx of God's light and love. We increase in wisdom and love through humility and a longing to learn and grow spiritually.

God is. Perhaps this statement sums it up best. We have tried to define, limit, understand, and explain God for millennia, but words are grossly inadequate. I exist because God is. There is no doubt in my mind. Alicia still exists, beyond the mere memories. Her radiant soul still shines upon us. I see her; I feel her presence; I know in unexplainable ways that her soul lives on. My choices are to accept this new relationship or deny it. I choose to accept it in its new form, and I find strength of faith by doing so. (Journal, August 27, 2002)

Changing Hues

What is real? What surreal?
The interplay from day to day.
Perception changes; life rearranges;
Joy to pain, then back again.

Eternal hope; yet, unsure how to cope
When tragedy falls and sadness calls?
Hope fades away, grief comes to stay;
Sadness ensues, endless blues.

Pain of loss, too much to bear.
Waning hope, utter despair.
I yearn for joy, for healing love,
My eyes implore the skies above.

Deep inside, hope doth abide,
Beyond the pain, love remains.
The struggle immense, somehow I sense
Healing love will come from above.

Somewhere beyond the pain;
The darkened skies and endless rain;
There lies a knowing, my soul is growing,
And wholeness will come once again.
(August 27, 2002)

Grieving Heart

The church bells chime in the distant Romanesque church. Sunday morning is such a peaceful time as the sun rises lazily in the eastern sky. The view from the courtyard of the Hotel Dei Castelli looks down over the sparkling blue water of the Mediterranean Sea along the shores of Sestra Levanti. Peace is in the air. One could be lulled into a feeling of serenity and the belief that all is well. Even though in my mind I know that God is in his/her place, in my heart, the pain screams for release. Alicia is missing, never to return. Her soul is alive and well, but my heart yearns for her presence.

The sun has just peeked through the magnificent trees as if to give me warmth and illumination, but I feel cold and numb inside. Will I ever feel the joyousness of life? Will I ever laugh fully and freely or feel the innocence of love again? I long for their return. My heart yearns for the exuberance of life to

*chase away the melancholy of death. Innocence and love have been stolen from
my heart, leaving the scars of violence and distrust. I long for peace within my
soul.* (September 1, 2002)

On returning from our first overseas experience, I felt compelled to look
through Alicia's personal papers, which she kept in an antique trunk
that now serves as an altar, covered with Alicia's pictures and memorabilia. After reading some cards and looking through some business
records, I came across a map of Italy with hand-drawn directions and
plans for a trip Alicia had evidently planned to take. Lo and behold, it
mirrored the trip that Bev and I had just completed through Venice,
Rome, Florence, Tuscany, and the Mediterranean Sea. Although we had
never talked about her plans, I was not surprised at the synchronicity.
I felt blessed by this confirmation of life after death, and fortunate for
her spiritual presence with us on the trip.

Chapter 23

Grief Knows No Bounds

The first anniversary of our daughter's murder was approaching. We had been invited to New York City for a day of remembrance, but it felt like a time of "show and tell" for the politicians who wanted to capitalize on this opportunity to display their "patriotism" and "compassion." We wanted no part of this exploitation and refused to be used by self-serving, disingenuous individuals who were hoping to pump up their votes as a result of our tragedy. Instead, we went to Montana to be with our family and to help celebrate our son Zac's birthday that same day. September 11: a day that will forever be bittersweet and tinged with tragedy.

We mustered our emotional and physical strength in an attempt to celebrate Zac's birth, but the shadow of death and feelings of loss hovered. Oh, we laughed, reminisced about happier times, shared stories about our son, and truly felt the glory of his birth and life, but the height of our joy would soon be overshadowed by the depth of our sorrow. The sadness could not be denied. The more we allowed ourselves to feel the joy of life, the more deeply we felt the pain. But to deny these feelings of love and joy only diminishes life, destining us for anguish and bitterness. I would not allow this to happen in my life. This was not what God willed for me or what my soul was destined to become.

Despite the pain, our time together with our family was healing and regenerating. Greg joined us, along with the rest of our immediate family. We played games, hiked, and rode dirt bikes through tree-lined paths and giant rock formations. We cooked together, talked, commiserated, reminisced, imbibed good wine, dined, and cried together, and the healing power of all of this time regenerated our souls and cleansed our hearts. Grieving is perhaps the greatest challenge one has to overcome in life. I could not have taken this painful journey alone.

Painful Reality

In many ways, the second year was harder than the first. I had convinced myself that the second year would somehow be easier to cope with. I was wrong. What I hadn't anticipated was the dissolution of the shock phase of grief, the protective mechanism that sheltered me from the devastation of my loss. The bluntness of the reality that Alicia was gone forever burned deeply. It was almost too much to take, but my faith deepened and I could feel Alicia, the angels, and God comforting me, strengthening me, healing me.

The time had come to go back to work. I was not looking forward to it. My heart was not in it, and I felt a calling to do something more with my life. I was being called to use my grief and work for the causes of peace and justice. I needed to make a positive difference in our world and help right the wrongs that had perpetuated the conditions leading to Alicia's murder.

It is either denial or ignorance to think that the U.S. bore no responsibility for the hatred that fueled the September 11 attacks. In many ways, the United States government has shirked its global responsibilities and allowed power and greed to guide its decisions. We befriended leaders in Saudi Arabia who funded the radical madrasas; we turned our backs on the genocide in Rwanda as the Hutus systematically killed the Tutsis, resulting in the deaths of one million people. When it served our purpose, we funded military operations in countries hostile to the United States. In Afghanistan, we supplied arms and intelligence for the Mujahadeen against the USSR, leaving the Taliban and warlords in power when we abandoned them, a country in ruins, after they defeated the USSR. We gave funding and weapons to Iraq and supported Saddam Hussein against Iran, only to have those weapons used against us. We provide millions of dollars in military aid to Israel while they bulldoze the houses of innocent people in the Gaza Strip and shoot Palestinian youth in the streets. We used depleted uranium in our bullets and missiles to fire on villages of innocent people in Iraq and Afghanistan. Compared to other world leaders, in relation to our per capita wealth, we supply only a pittance to alleviate world hunger and disease, spending billions on our military complex and our own weapons of mass destruction while thousands of children die of starvation and illness each day. Our arrogance at the expense of human compassion merely perpetuates more hate and violence. My daughter was caught in the crossfire.

It is time to reevaluate our priorities, elect leaders who have a vision based on wisdom and compassion, and change our attitude before we too become victims of our own short-sightedness. History has many lessons to offer us in this regard—think of the Roman Empire for instance. Peace can only be had in conjunction with justice. Justice cannot be had as long as an elite few possess the majority of the world's wealth while half the world's population lives in abject poverty.

How have we come to this juncture? What motivates human beings to want to kill other human beings? How can the Osama bin Ladens of the world justify the targeting and killing of innocent people? How can "civilized" countries justify the killing of innocent civilians who just happen to be in the way? Many in our country proclaim with self-righteous indignation that we are God's chosen ones, that such carnage is somehow justified because of what "they" did to us. I wonder how they would feel if their daughter were murdered in retaliation for our aggressive actions. Perhaps they would react with greater vengeance—but maybe, just maybe, they would hear the call to clarity and understanding and respond with greater compassion.

According to the Lancet Study, which came out in the fall of 2004, over 100,000 Iraqi civilians had at that point died as a result of the United States' most recent military action in Iraq. This claim was vehemently challenged by the Republican administration because of the pending presidential election, but, oddly enough, the group responsible for the study had previously been used by our government for other studies; their results were always considered reliable. The Bush administration made a concerted effort to downplay the civilian casualties caused by the Iraq and Afghanistan conflicts and soften the harsh reality of the devastating effects these conflicts wrought upon our troops and our national resources.

The real travesty is the devastation of human lives that has resulted from our "war of mass deception." The billions of dollars spent on mass destruction could have been better used for mass construction—efforts to alleviate the unjust conditions in our world and demonstrate human compassion rather than perpetuate more hatred. As a world leader, this is America's higher calling. And all of this is being done in the shadow of the reality that our actions in Iraq are unjust and unfounded, based upon the conjured specter of "weapons of mass destruction" and unproven ties to the attacks of September 11. People of America, wake up, before your children become victims of the next generation of terrorists—terrorists we have helped to create.

Chapter 24

An Eye for an Eye

Alicia was a wise soul who recognized the interconnection of all of life. She reacted with heartfelt compassion when she witnessed injustice, poverty, and suffering. She loved to travel the world and spread joy and hope to those who felt neither; and she reached out to those in need. Alicia had the innate ability to identify and relate to the divine within each and every person she met, empowering them with a sense of the goodness of life and hope for the future. How ironic that her life would be taken by those she had striven to help!

I have stated before in these pages my belief that all of life is deeply intertwined; those things we do to others, we do also to ourselves. We, individually and collectively, must learn to treat others with a sense of positive regard, no matter what their position in life, religious creed, socio-economic status, handicap, color, sexual preference...and the list goes on. The love, compassion, and understanding that we share—or, conversely, the hate, vengeance, and lack of understanding we project onto others—will come back to us in some way, someday. As Mahatma Gandhi so wisely stated, "An eye for an eye makes the whole world blind."

Many people don't seem to grasp this very basic concept, while at the same time they proclaim to be children of God or Allah. Prior to the United States' invasion of Iraq, I was having a discussion with a family member who vehemently maintained that we should indeed go forward with this war, mainly because the Iraqis "don't believe in Jesus Christ" and are therefore "sinners." Osama bin Laden justified the attacks on America as an attack on the "infidels" and felt directed by Allah to rid the world of infidels. Who is right? What would Jesus have done? What would Mohammed have done?

Many times I have heard the question asked of our invasion of Iraq, "Who would Jesus have bombed?" Some people aren't able to take the ego out of such decisions or deal with the fear that drives them to react with such vengeance. While they envision the destruction of an enemy with the face of Osama bin Laden or Saddam Hussein, I envision the face of an innocent child dying in her mother's arms. I ended the conversation with my family member about the invasion of Iraq by stating, "My God is a God of love and understanding, not one of death and destruction."

Speaking Out for Peace

In the latter part of the first year after Alicia's death, I began speaking out about my thoughts on the war, America's policies in regard to developing countries, poverty, disease, justice and peace. I wrote articles in the newspaper, sent emails, and made phone calls to our congressional representatives and President Bush; participated in documentaries; talked at public forums; visited classrooms and talked with college students; presented at workshops; interviewed with TV reporters; and occasionally attended antiwar protests. I soon realized that I had much to say and that it came from a place of wisdom heretofore untapped. I had awakened to my moral authority. I watched my extended family as they tried to comprehend this new outspokenness, knowing that they believed it was just a phase prompted by grief. Recently, my brother asked me if I felt "called" to the causes of peace and justice—in other words, how deeply committed was I to this cause? I told him that I had never been surer of anything in my life. The veil of ignorance had been lifted and clarity had appeared. Now I needed to speak out or forever hold my peace.

Around this time we became aware of September 11th Families for a Peaceful Tomorrow, a group I mentioned earlier that consisted of 9/11 families who felt the same way we did. I felt affirmed in my convictions and intrigued by the strong correlation of our messages. I felt compelled to reach out to other victims of violence, particularly the Afghani and Iraqi families who had borne the brunt of America's vengeance. Unlike us, they had nowhere to turn for help, no hope for relief, and they had lived with poverty and war for decades. Peaceful Tomorrows members traveled to Afghanistan, witnessed the suffering firsthand, and talked with the victims. Many of the children who had survived the attacks were suffering from posttraumatic stress disorder and were permanently scarred and disabled, both emotionally and physically.

In the documentary that resulted from this encounter, I recognized the searing pain of loss on the face of a mother as she talked about

losing eight members of her family and her home to the United States'
bombings. She had nothing. When she went to the American consulate
for help, she was turned away and called a beggar. It would be months,
if ever, before she received aid: relief efforts were slow and cumbersome
in coming and designed not for expediency but to optimize its public
relations impact. I felt deep compassion for those poor Afghani people.
They had suffered for years, and the future didn't look much brighter.

Chapter 25

Not in my Daughter's Name!

Losing a child is bitterly painful. The full weight of the grief, the pain, the intense sadness, the utter despair, and the crushing depression were all too real. The weight of the world was upon us. I thought my heart was going to break apart. Bev felt the same way. Some days we felt we could hardly go on. There was no escape. And there didn't seem to be much hope of it getting better.

In the early stages of grief there is a protective veil that provides shelter from the powerful emotions that are coiled to strike. Family and friends are more intimately connected in the period shortly after a loss, but after a while, life goes on for everyone else. Bev and I were left alone in our despair. There were days when life was utterly oppressive, but knowing that our loved ones needed us, especially our children and grandchildren, kept us going.

The endless days trudged on. The pain seemed to take on a renewed strength of its own as the depression settled in like a dark cloud. Each day seemed like a chore, and the joie de vivre from my previous life prior to 9/11 felt like a distant dream. Each day I would read the news and listen to reports from around the world, all of them centered on the unending death and destruction, by-products of war; many of them made reference to September 11. There wasn't a day that went by that I didn't hear, see, or read about 9/11. I was especially sensitive to any reference to the date and was quick to jump in if people used it to rationalize the ongoing killing in Afghanistan and Iraq. My heart screamed for cessation from this insanity. *Not in my daughter's name!* I cried out silently. *We must stop this senseless killing.*

Through the pain and sadness compassion had filled my heart and a sense of spiritual enlightenment was making its way into my life. I could not ignore it.

Alicia's Last Visit Home—June 11, 2001

Grandma, Alicia, Mom (Bev) 2001

....

Chapter 26

....

Ten Years Afterward

It has been nearly a decade since Alicia was murdered—truly, a heart-wrenching journey. There have, however, been moments of enlightenment along with the constant pain and sorrow. Thankfully, Bev and I have been gifted with incredible love along the way. Looking back, I feel truly blessed to have such caring family and friends, and my faith in a loving God has been strengthened. Those who have never experienced such a horrific tragedy and painful loss firsthand cannot comprehend the impact, the incredible heartache and the deep-seated sadness. I couldn't possibly expect them to understand.

For Bev and me, along with our children, it has been ten years of painful healing, ten years of desolate sadness, ten years of learning how to live life without our daughter and sister, ten years of tumultuous war as a result of 9/11, and ten years of yearning for peace and justice for our world. We have spent ten years soul searching and learning how to feel joy and hope once again. Yet somehow, by allowing ourselves to feel the depths of our sorrow, deeper love and empathy have come to life. Grandchildren have been born, our daughter and nieces and nephews have married, we've traveled and created new adventures, familial love has flourished, friends have been there for us along the way, and joy has returned to our hearts. Through the grace of God, life's goodness shines through the darkness. Hope does spring eternal.

Alicia's spiritual presence has given us strength, for she was (and is) a loving presence and a wizened soul. She lived her life as if she somehow knew that there would be no tomorrow. She experienced the joy of life to its fullest, and she made the world a better place with her presence here. Believe me, it has been a difficult and painful journey without her in our lives. We find strength in the way she lived her life, which has given us courage and hope to labor through the pain and sorrow of losing such a beautiful soul. Memories of her comfort us in untold ways, and her soul continues to shine a light in the darkness.

When I reminisce about time spent with my daughter, I am awed by her ongoing spiritual presence, her profound and inquisitive nature, and the deep abiding compassion and love she manifested while physically with us. I am blessed to have fathered such an evolved soul. I had always assumed that we would live our lives out in a natural progression: her marriage and the birth of her children, lots of family time, travel together, new adventures, the unveiling of life's mysteries and the growth of our love as we aged together. I thoroughly enjoyed Alicia's company when she became an adult, reveling in our shared adventures and the many philosophical conversations we had, contentious as they were at times. We challenged each other in ways that enhanced our growth. More importantly, we learned how to enjoy each other's company beyond the parent-child relationship. I was looking forward to a lifetime of her companionship. Her time on this earth was too fleeting.

Immediately after we received the devastating news of her death, through the intense pain and overwhelming sadness, I felt the comfort of a divine presence within. I could also feel Alicia's presence and, on occasion, I was able to gaze upon her angelic face as she drew near. I knew I could not allow myself to become bitter and resentful, even though anger is a part of the grieving process. Early on, I felt the seeds of forgiveness take hold, but I wasn't sure what to do with them at the time. I still had much grieving to do. Many times I felt confused and unsure. So, I did as I had learned to do as a child: I prayed. My prayers, at first, were desperate pleas for help, but they soon became honest, heartfelt requests for understanding, for hope, and for peace. It was as if the weight of the world had fallen upon my shoulders and I would either buckle under the pressure or learn to carry the load. I am still learning to carry it, and it is making me stronger.

I didn't understand all of the dynamics behind Alicia's murder; I was fairly ignorant of the underlying political ramifications; I knew virtually nothing about Osama bin Laden and al Qaeda; I had very little meaningful grasp of Islam; and I wasn't sure how to sort all of this out in terms of justice, peace, or war while in the throes of grief. I knew, however, that I was totally opposed to any vengeful response that would cause the killing of more innocent people. I conveyed this very clearly to the media hounds who sought us out after 9/11, but the message was often lost in the quagmire of their own politicized agendas.

I allowed myself time to grieve, as I knew it was both unavoidable and essential to the healing process. But soon I was on a mission. I felt compelled to do what I could to help the healing of America, knowing that a deadly military response, founded in fear and fueled by anger, would only exacerbate the root problem and make it worse. It became clear that America had to find a way to bring those responsible for 9/11 to justice in an international court of law. The eyes of the world were upon us, and we needed to demonstrate to the world that we would not sink to the level of the terrorists who perpetrated these heinous crimes against humanity. But al Qaeda had baited the trap, and America would soon take the bait. Osama bin Laden hoped to lure America into an unwinnable war on their turf, and our politicians reacted as expected. Not surprisingly, I would soon discover that the Bush administration had already decided to press for war in Iraq prior to 9/11, as outlined by the Project for the New American Century[4]; the attacks of September 11 fit neatly into their plan.

I dedicated my life to understanding all I could about the underlying issues, the hidden agendas, the mindset of Osama bin Laden and terrorism in general, the politics and politicians, and the history behind all of it. Now, when I talk about these issues of peace, war, justice, politics, terrorism, or related issues, I am able to speak with some understanding and a certain degree of "moral authority" that comes from my own experience, not just raw emotion. Many people have strong opinions about these issues, but few have much depth of understanding about or personal experience with them. This lack of understanding becomes extremely problematic in a democracy where politicians are elected by the public, many members of which are misinformed or uninformed about vitally important issues. Politicians know how to rally the uninformed masses around single emotional issues such as abortion, health care, homosexuality, religious beliefs, and fear of the unknown while glossing over other, less marketable issues. It is our duty to question our country's leaders and to become as informed as we possibly can on all issues, looking beyond the biased messages of the politicized media and the twisted communications of politicians and lobbyists.

It's easy to get frustrated in the world of politics, and it's often hard to discern truth. Millions of dollars are spent on influencing the minds of the voters, and with the recent Supreme Court decision to open the floodgates for campaign contributions, the sky is the limit financially. Another case in point is a well-known tactic originally developed by the CIA under George H. W. Bush to influence the perceptions of the people in other countries is to construct a tag line, a succinct, pointed message, and repeatedly present it in a variety of forms as the truth. This implants the message in the memory center of the brain, and

---

4   The Project for the New American Century was a Washington D.C. think tank created to influence the United States government in several key areas, including the overthrow of Saddam Hussein, and create a strong military presence in the Middle East to protect our vested interests. Members included Dick Cheney, Donald Rumsfeld, Jeb Bush, Paul Wolfowitz, Richard Armitage, John Bolton, and other Bush administration officials.

soon people begin believing it to be the truth. This tactic was used very effectively by the Bush administration in the lead-up to the Iraq war. We heard over and over again from Bush, Cheney, Rice, Rumsfeld, Powell, Rove, and others about Saddam Hussein's "weapons of mass destruction," which were known to be nonexistent; about "chemical warfare" and mobile chemical warehouses, which were fictional; about the purported purchase of yellowcake uranium from Niger, a story that came from falsified documents; about the "white cloud of destruction," an image that created visions of a nuclear bomb, which Iraq did not have the capability of making...and the list goes on. The administration knew these assertions to be false, but they created fear in the American public, making it possible to move ahead with the Project for the New American Century and expand the "war on terrorism" against Iraq that was actually unrelated to 9/11. Though there was no known connection between 9/11 and Iraq, the Bush administration systematically used the horror of 9/11 to elicit fear and gain support for an unjust war. A "war on terrorism" is open-ended and unwinnable because there is no clear-cut enemy. Now, after nearly ten years of war and virtually no progress in reducing terrorism at a tremendous cost of human life and money, perhaps even the supporters of this war can see how wrong that decision was—or they will continue to keep their heads in the sand. Truth and honesty have become victims of the war on terrorism.

Though sidetracked by President Clinton's sexual indiscretions and a Congress hell-bent on impeachment, the Clinton administration recognized the threat against America posed by al Qaeda and Osama bin Laden during the late nineties and attempted to eliminate the threat, mostly by covert action. It soon became evident that bin Laden was behind the attacks on American embassies in Nairobi and Tanzania—attacks that had specifically targeted Americans. The CIA had already been tracking bin Laden's movements, and much discussion at all levels of national security centered on the growing threat that bin Laden and al Qaeda posed to America and how to eliminate it. In August of 1998, seventy-five Tomahawk missiles slammed into Zawhar Kili, a meeting place where senior leaders of Islamist militant and terrorist groups linked to bin Laden, along with bin Laden himself, had planned to meet. As it turned out, bin Laden had been alerted by (presumably) Pakistani intelligence and departed before the strike. Efforts continued to capture or eliminate bin Laden and the growing threat to America. Bin Laden and Mullah Omar had issued fatwas[5] against Americans, both civilian and military. Plans to use commercial jets as missiles were already in progress. A strike on American soil was inevitable, and our government knew it.

---

5   "Declaration of War against the Americans Occupying the Land of the Two Holy Places."

In the summer of 2001, terrorist alert indicators were "blinking red,"[6] according to CIA reports. The Clinton administration had made the threat of terrorism and national security a top priority for the incoming Bush administration, only to have their priorities arrogantly dismissed. Presentations by Sandy Berger (Clinton's National Security Advisor) and Richard Clarke (terrorism czar in both the Clinton and Bush administrations) specifically outlined the threat of attack by al Qaeda and stressed the necessity of immediate action. In the year 2000, the Clinton administration had ordered two U.S. Navy submarines to stay on station in the northern Arabian Sea, ready to attack if bin Laden's coordinates were found.[11] Indicators of a pending attack against America became increasingly clear to all who were involved in discerning intelligence in the late nineties and early in the Bush presidency. Case in point: the FAA had sent over sixty memoranda to the airlines in the ninety-day period before September 11, 2001, alerting them to the terrorist plot involving the hijacking of commercial planes, using them as missiles, and flying them into major U.S. political and economic landmarks. At the same time, the FBI had discovered Arabic men with terrorist ties training to fly commercial jets in Phoenix in the summer of 2001; in August of 2001 the FBI also arrested Zacarias Moussaoui, who had been training to be a pilot of one of these hijacked planes in a flight school in Minneapolis, and discovered that he had established ties to the 9/11 terrorists and al Qaeda (information that would be altered and minimized by an FBI supervisor prior to 9/11). Additionally, an al Qaeda operative who had been selected to complete the pilot training in preparation for the 9/11 attacks defected to the FBI a year before the attack and revealed the plot to attack America with hijacked commercial planes.

It was becoming obvious to the intelligence community that an attack on the United States of America using our own commercial jets as missiles was being planned. The situation was coming to a head in late summer of 2001, at the same time that President George W. Bush decided to take a month-long vacation on his Texas ranch. He had to have known that this was a critical time for national security and that an attack on America was pending. By this point, it was increasingly clear to the intelligence community. Daily memos were going to the President stressing the pending attacks.

So, why did the Bush administration not make this a priority? "Terrorism wasn't on their plate of key issues," said a former Clinton White House official.[12] But why did they act as if they had been so completely unaware of this possibility after we were attacked, even though they knew who had attacked us on the same day? Why did

---

6   The "blinking red" reference comes from a statement that Tenet made to the 9/11 Commission in 2004 in reference to the intelligence world in the summer of 2001.[1]

Condoleezza Rice say to the public with such feigned innocence, a few weeks after September 11, that they had had no idea that hijackers would steal planes and crash them into buildings, when in fact they did have intelligence that specified this? This plot had been spawned by "Project Bojinka" in 1995 and masterminded by Ramzi Yousef[13], a known al Qaeda terrorist,[7] and it was rapidly coming to fruition in the summer of 2001.

When all the facts are laid on the table, it's easy to conclude that the Bush administration was either totally inept, blinded by its own agenda, or, as some have suggested, complicit in the attacks. I'm not a conspiracy theorist, but given all the evidence, it's hard to understand why they didn't take action. With evidence of a pending attack mounting throughout the months leading up to September 11, why did the Bush administration wait until September 4, 2001 to convene their first meeting addressing these issues?

Some would say that all of the above is merely speculative, or that hindsight is 20/20; some would dismiss it entirely as a grieving father's speculation. But the facts are painfully revealing: this tragedy should have been prevented.

All we, the 9/11 families, wanted was an unbiased, transparent investigation that would include the full scope of the intelligence leading up to 9/11; the politics that led to a breakdown in our country's security; exposure of the financiers behind the terrorist plot, which included some noted Saudis; and a complete understanding of the Saudi connection (fifteen of the hijackers were Saudis). We wanted to know: how our dependence on oil had factored into the decision for war, the timelines of known facts leading up to the attack of 9/11, and reasons for our government's failure to take preventive action—in other words, why wasn't the attack on America on 9/11 prevented? And why was the Bush administration so gung ho about waging war on Iraq, which

---

7   "Western secret services knew as far back as 1995 that suspected terror mastermind Osama bin Laden planned to attack civilian sites using commercial passenger planes." Quoting sources "close to western intelligence agencies," the newspaper reported that: "The plan was discovered in January 1995 by Philippine police who were investigating a possible attack against Pope John Paul II on a visit to Manila..."

"They found details of the plan in a computer seized in an apartment used by three men who were part of Bin Laden's al-Qaeda network. It provided for 11 planes to be exploded simultaneously by bombs placed on board, but also in an alternative form for several planes flying to the United States to be hijacked and flown into civilian targets. Among targets mentioned was the World Trade Center in New York, which was destroyed in the September 11 terror attacks in the United States that killed thousands."

"The plan has been masterminded by one Ramzi Yousef, who was arrested in Islamabad in the wake of Murad's interrogation. Both Murad and Yousef were extradited to the United States, tried and convicted for complicity in the 1993 attack on the WTC. The date of Yousef's conviction was 11 September 1996. From that point, given the fascination terrorists have with anniversaries, 11 September should surely have become a watch date."

had nothing to do with 9/11? The main responsibility of the American government is to protect its citizens. They failed miserably on 9/11, and I, as the father of one of the victims, have a right to know why. The American people have a right to know why.

Chapter 27

The Return of Joy

Grief involving murder and politics is complicated. Losing someone you expect to lose, such as a grandparent or even a parent, is painful enough, but often expected. I lost my father last June, and although I am still sad and I miss him, grieving his death has been easier to accept and much less complicated. He was in failing health and I had the opportunity to spend time with him before he died. Death was a relief from his suffering. We had a body to mourn over. With Alicia, we didn't even have a shard of bone. Early in our grieving, we even fantasized that she had somehow escaped and was unable to get home. Of course it wasn't rational, but it allowed us some sense of hope.

One of the byproducts of intensive grief is that it forces us to scrutinize all aspects of our lives. While grieving, I questioned everything: God, religious beliefs, government, political motivations, injustice, world poverty, the media, our country's values, my own personal values, relationships, health and well-being... I no longer let fear stop me from speaking my mind or having informed but controversial opinions that were counter to the mainstream. I felt emboldened. At the same time, I felt a deep humility. I longed for answers, for truth, for justice, for hope, for peace. I felt a deep, abiding compassion and a newfound sense of responsibility for those who have suffered injustices in our world. I felt the deep connection with all of life more completely. I searched deeper into my own soul for truth, for hope and for peace. I found forgiveness. Forgiveness has a regenerative power that connects us more deeply to God and to each other. It allows us to let go of the anger, the hatred and the need for vengeance. It doesn't preclude the need for justice, nor does it sanction the actions of those responsible for evil deeds. It did allow me to heal and find peace in my soul.

Amazingly, as I grieved I witnessed the boundaries of my own being dissipate; I felt intricately connected with the Divine in all of life. My left-hemisphere ego was subdued and my "right mind" flourished. In these moments, I could almost grasp conceptually the reasons that allowed the bin Laden's of the world to exist and to perpetuate such evil. We intuitively have within us the ability to discern truth beyond the ego mind. We are given a modicum of free will, but there are forces at work that influence us in unseen ways toward good or evil. We choose, from our own rational mind in accordance with our defining love, either self-serving or "other" serving love, the course of which we will follow. It is too simplistic and naive to think that an omnipotent God is pulling all the strings like a puppet master and that this life is all predetermined. That way we don't have to own our behaviors and make the necessary changes. We can just blame God.

Never once in my grief have I blamed God for Alicia's murder. Never once along this sad and lonely journey did I lose faith in a wise and loving God. In fact, I felt God's loving presence more completely than ever, guiding me, consoling me, filling my heart with love. At times I lost faith in my fellow human beings. In a moment of clarity, I came to realize that we are all only human, and being human requires that we choose between good and evil; we have the freedom to learn and to love, or to make mistakes and to choose actions that are hateful. If we choose our actions from a self-serving, egocentric love, we perpetuate evil; if we act in accordance with divine love and wisdom for the good of the "other," we align ourselves with God's will for us. The self-serving ego must be kept in check to allow the grace of God to manifest in us. Grief has a way of dissolving the ego and opening our hearts to a greater love, but we still have to make choices, even in the midst of the pain, sadness, and turmoil that abounds.

Life, at least on this plane, ended for Alicia. But, for me and my remaining loved ones, it continues on, albeit in a new form. I realized early in my grief that life would never be the same, that at some level I would always feel a deep sadness. I've learned to accept this reality and, in some way, to embrace it. To deny it would be to deny the tremendous love I have for Alicia.

At the beginning of my grief journey, I questioned whether I would ever feel joy again. Many times, when joy would manifest, it would be followed by overwhelming sadness. Now I can honestly say that I feel joy in its purity, and I cherish its return. At other times, I feel the abiding sadness of my loss in its fullest, but I'm okay with that. It doesn't consume my life as it once did. It's always there, in my heart and in my soul, and I have learned to honor that graciously. By allowing myself to feel the fullness of the sadness and pain, I have increased my capacity for love and compassion. It's amazing how that works! When I try to stuff down my pain and deny my sadness, I feel numb. Consequently, my capacity for love is diminished and I feel half alive. I cannot and will not live my life like that.

When I look back over the last ten years, I am deeply saddened by yet utterly amazed at this journey of grief I've been on—amazed that I have survived such an overpowering and dark force, a force that has the potential to destroy. Within that latent power of grief is also a regenerative force that wills us toward greater love and deeper under-standing. This is truly the grace of God. This restorative power is much greater than the destructive force that lurks during times of despair and vulnerability. Even at my lowest points, when life seemed deso-late and oppressive, I could see a distant light beckoning me onward. I absolutely knew that this was the Divine Presence willing me on. This was God's presence within.

I share my experience knowing that some will continue to doubt the whole concept of God. Religion has not helped its own cause in the understanding of such matters. Somewhere along the way, spiritual reflections and religious thinking have become foreign to many left-brain dominant thinkers. But herein lies the problem: if we try to com-prehend the concept of God merely from our logical, rational, left brain, the ego will lead us astray. The concepts of God, the interconnection of all of life, and consequently compassion, love, and joy reside in the "right mind" or the right hemisphere. Our culture relies heavily on logic and deductive reasoning and devalues the power and beauty of the conceptual, creative aspect of our brains. Each of us needs to find the optimal balance between the two in order to live life to the fullest and actualize even a portion of our potential as spiritual beings. There is no way to fully understand logically the murder of Alicia. The ego-directed left brain will lead us down the path of self-destruction, into the abyss, if allowed to reign unchecked. Anger, blame, revenge, power, greed, and fear are all tools of the ego (or the devil, some might say) to keep us trapped, to convince us to rely on our own perceived power while refut-ing the omnipotence and omnipresence of a wise and loving creator.

I remember distinctly when I first realized that untainted joy had returned to my life. It was in the fourth year after Alicia's death. I cher-ished the sensation, the ecstatic feeling, and the relief of knowing that the gift of joy was mine once again. Life without joy soon becomes unbearable. We are made to feel joy as we are created to feel love; they come from the selfsame wellspring.

Chapter 28

"Be the Change"

Throughout my grief journey, I continued to speak at different venues on issues related to peace and justice. I really felt strongly that my voice could make a difference. I continued my involvement in September 11th Families for Peaceful Tomorrows, whose name comes from a speech by the Reverend Dr. Martin Luther King, Jr. in which he said, "...the past is prophetic in that wars are poor chisels for carving out peaceful tomorrows."

I was invited to join renowned author, spiritual leader, social activist, and world lecturer Marianne Williamson, a wise, wonderful, and loving person, to share my experience at the Sunday morning worship service at the Department of Peace Conference in Washington D.C. on September 11, 2005. I do not see myself as a public speaker. I become anxious and my voice quivers at times. But I feel passionate about my message, and I sense that it has redeeming value.

I didn't cherish the idea of presenting my thoughts and feelings in front of five hundred people alongside such an accomplished speaker. It was a bit overwhelming, to say the least! While being introduced, I performed deep breathing exercises to calm my nervousness. The conference included incredible speakers, such as Marianne Williamson, Dr. Patch Adams, Azim Khamisa, Barbara Marx Hubbard, Ambassador John McDonald, Walter Cronkite, and Congressman Dennis Kucinich, along with others, and I was awed by their presence. Needless to say, I was a bit nervous and, because of the deeply personal nature of my message, emotionally distraught when my turn came.

Thankfully, I was able to deliver my message without hyperventilating. Several people approached me afterward to tell me it had inspired and moved them. Marianne's message of hope afterward was filled with compassion and understanding. She is truly a wizened soul. One of the things I remember as so astute from Marianne's talk was when her comment about the deep commitment the hijackers had to their cause—a commitment so great that they were willing to do whatever it took to imprint their will on the human race, even though it was evil, wicked, violent, cruel, and unimaginably horrible. In contrast, many of us who have love in our hearts are "kinda, sorta, when it's convenient, committed to love." She said that there are many more people on this planet who have love in their hearts than hate, yet it is as if hate has a grip on our planet. When enough of us are convicted enough to love, when we achieve a critical mass with strong enough convictions for the cause of love, that is when we will turn it around.[14] This not only requires deep conviction, but also a humble heart and an openness to the Lord's will for us.

I love the quote from Gandhi that says, "Be the change you wish to see in the world." We must be willing to put our convictions into action or sit by passively and let the dark forces of evil have their way. This speaks to the whole concept of Swedenborg's concept of "uses" I have referenced throughout my writings. "Our uses in which we participate in the common good is the Lord acting through us."[15] "...Being human means to do uses from the Lord to the neighbor for His sake."[16]

Death sharpens our view of the world. When Alicia was killed, it felt as if the blinders had been pulled from my eyes. I could no longer sit back and expect others to change this messed-up world of ours, a world that could provide for all of humanity's basic needs if only we humans made it a priority, a world that accepts the killing of innocent people as a necessary evil that comes with war, a world in which thirty to forty thousand children die every day due to lack of food, shelter, and treatable disease; a world in which the rich keep getting richer and the poor get poorer and the "haves" hide their heads in the sand to avoid feeling guilty while the "have-nots" suffer needlessly, a world in which discrimination is still common practice and sanctioned by many, a world in which people view their neighbors with distrust and often contempt. As long as blatant injustice is allowed to exist and atrocities are permitted to continue, there will be no lasting peace. We cannot sit on the world's largest stockpile of nuclear weapons and other weapons of mass destruction, enough to destroy this planet, and expect other countries to succumb meekly to our power. As long as we spend our abundant wealth on the machinery of war while ignoring the needs of the billions who are suffering needlessly, there will be no peace. We have to ask ourselves this: is the warring world we've created, fraught with injustice, distrust, and contempt, the world we want to hand over to our grandchildren? That is, if they survive.

I believe there are many people in this world with good intentions and love in their hearts. But do their actions really speak to that goodness? Is there consistency between their supposed compassion and their daily deeds? Perhaps it's a conceptual matter: where does our individual responsibility stop, and where does it begin? Do we believe in the interconnection of all life, or are we separate beings with no responsibility for the other? Are we our brothers' keepers? Do we bear some responsibility for the ills of the world—and, ultimately, for the solution? Or do we just blame it on the Democrats or the Republicans, or the Muslims or the Jews, or the Christians, the Buddhists, the Hindus . . . or God? As long as we are blaming others, we can simply exonerate ourselves of any guilt or responsibility, which negates any possibility of change. Simply seeing the world through the narrow lens of our own needs goes against the tenets of most major religions and what our loving Creator wills for us. It is time to own up to our responsibilities as individuals and as a nation. If this country is truly to be called a world leader, then we need to lead with wisdom, understanding, compassion, and love. If we don't and we continue in our policies of power and greed, we will surely fall, just as the Roman Empire did.

In 2006, I was invited to speak in Italy at the Alleati per la Pace, a national peace alliance held in Riccione in the Rimini Province. As a part of this trip, we were asked to speak in secondary schools and public forums and to meet with the media. I was fascinated to note that many of the high-school-age students I spoke to knew more about American politics than our own high school students—and many of our college students. They asked probing questions about the legitimacy of the war in Iraq, about the political motivations behind it, about its worldwide repercussions, about the devastating effects it was having on civilians, and more. Many could not understand how, in a democracy where, according to opinion polls, the majority of the electorate opposed the war, we could allow it to go on. Why had we reelected President Bush when so many opposed his war?

At the time, I worked in a college setting in Michigan as an administrator and had given presentations and led discussions with many college and high school students around the U.S., but I had never encountered such thoughtful and pointed questions. Sadly, throughout our travels, we encountered individuals who were under the impression that the Bush administration had been complicit in the attacks of September 11, 2001 to further their own agenda. According to opinion polls, many in our own country believe this also.

Chapter 29

Culpability and the Victim's Compensation Fund

One of the other major issues we had to contend with as a part of our grief journey was whether to accept the government pay-off, or "hush money," as I called it, 7 billion dollars from the Victims Compensation Fund. This was taxpayer money that the Bush administration and congress decided to pay out to the 9/11 victims' families with the stipulation that, if you accepted it, you would not be able to take legal action against those who might be culpable. Many families, left in a bind after their spouses or other loved ones were killed, chose to accept this money. I can certainly empathize and understand. There was a lot of pressure from the government to accept this "generous offer." Timelines were given, phone calls were made, meetings were set up, all in the name of helping us make the "right decision": to accept the money and not make waves.

Life had become painfully difficult and vastly confusing and it was hard even to make day-to-day decisions, let alone a major decision such as this. The offer of compensation without legal battles seemed like the path of least resistance. But many questions remained unanswered. A cover-up of vital information by our government had become painfully evident; there was strong resistance by the Bush administration to investigate the causal factors and bureaucratic failures that had allowed this plot to unfold. I wanted answers.

Not only were there blatant failures to take action to prevent this tragedy at the highest level of the government, but there were also obvious failures at every level. NORAD (North American Aerospace Defense Command) scheduled wargames for the morning of September 11 and was ordered to stand down by Vice President Cheney as

American Airlines Flight 77 made its way toward the Pentagon. Airport security allowed the hijackers onboard with mace, knives, box cutters, and possibly bombs and guns, according to reports from the planes themselves, and some of the hijackers were on a terrorist watch list when they boarded the planes. Even though the hijackers set off the security alarms at airport security, they were not searched, nor were their bags opened, according to airport security videos. The airlines had been alerted over sixty times about the pending attack in the prior three months by the FAA, and it was common knowledge that a hijacking plot was in the planning stages and rapidly coming to a conclusion. The intelligence indicators were "blinking red" according to reports, which meant that the plot to attack the United States was imminent. It's hard to understand why the airlines did not alert the pilots, flight crews, or airport security about any of this beforehand. Did economic interests rule their decision? It certainly did with Boeing, the maker of these airplanes. They had been fined and mandated to change the cockpit doors on these airliners on several occasions, so that a potential hijacker could not have access to the cockpits. Instead, they chose to pay the fines when they were found guilty of negligence, and saved money by doing so.

These revelations, together with the secrecy rampant at the highest levels of government, prompted Bev and me, along with one hundred other victim's families, to take legal action. We wanted answers. We wanted accountability for the blatant failures, and we wanted to ensure that measures would be taken to address the systemic problems that had allowed this devious plot to unfold. This was not an easy decision. I had never sued anyone and probably never would have, but this was my daughter's life and I had a right to know the whole truth.

We were determined to see this through and sought the services of a very reputable law firm who was representing other 9/11 families; it had successfully taken on the tobacco industry years before. Our attorneys were very sensitive to our feelings and needs, wanted to see that justice was served, and were not in it for their own financial gain. They spent more money investigating all the aspects of the 9/11 attacks than they could ever recoup from a favorable ruling. They uncovered information that was deliberately being hidden or altered by our government and intelligence agencies for various political reasons under the auspices of "national security." They diligently investigated causal factors, culpability, inconsistencies, sources of funding, and other aspects until we had answers to many of our questions, ugly as they were.

It's not easy to accept that trusted officials misrepresented the truth, blatantly lying in some cases. It took me awhile to come to forgiveness. I prayed fervently for those in charge, that they might be brought to a place of wisdom and be made to feel compassion in vital decisions yet to be made. But forgiveness does not preclude accountability.

The years went on; the wheels of justice move very slowly. We provided all the information about Alicia and our family requested by our attorneys. We participated in hearings and relived the trauma of 9/11 over and over again. We met with the defendants' representatives and lawyers, appeared in front of a federal judge, and persevered throughout the process of mediation, ad nauseam. The "defendants" had an endless stream of funding, strong lobbying power, a team of sharp lawyers, and a strategy to prolong this process as long as they could. They knew that this was an extremely emotional issue for us and we would eventually wear down. For them, it was just business as usual. We knew that we had enough evidence to win the case but, over time, our will was weakening. We were emotionally spent.

After several years of this emotional marathon, we decided that enough was enough. Grieving was hard enough without all the legal mumbo jumbo, so we accepted a settlement. We knew that others would see this through to the end, but for us, it was just too painful. We needed to heal and get on with our lives. We had answers to many of our questions, but felt compromised by our efforts to gain full accountability and justice. Perhaps we never would have anyway.

The settlement would never make up for the murder of our daughter and no amount of money in the world would make it right, but it did allow us some financial relief that we would not have had otherwise. We were able to provide a nest egg for our children and grandchildren, pay off all our bills, buy a home, travel, perform random acts of kindness, and retire to spend more time with family and work for peace and justice. But money was never the issue. We wanted to ensure that changes occurred at all levels so that such a horrific tragedy would never happen again. Some changes have resulted when it comes to airline safety and security issues. But our country's actions in response to 9/11 have not addressed the underlying problems that led to the attack in the first place. By our bellicose actions, we have created more hostility, helping to produce and recruit more angry young terrorists willing to join al Qaeda and like organizations who hate the United States. In addition, we have severely damaged the infrastructures of two countries, displaced millions of people from their homes, and killed and wounded hundreds of thousands of people, including our own service men and women. Was this approach the best way to eradicate the hatred for America? Is this our vision for peace and justice? Does this seem divinely inspired or sanctioned by a loving God?

Peace is not something we can kill our way into. Peace is not a place we can come to through the ego mind. Peace is the presence of the Divine within each of us; it's a feeling of interrelatedness in which we feel the interconnection of all life with God. Is peace attainable in the midst of abounding confusion, chaos, hate, and animosity? Not if we allow fear to direct our course. Not if we make decisions that feed the ego's need for power and greed. Not if we continue on the path of destruction. I have been shown a deep abiding peace, even in the midst of tragedy. If I can find inner peace, anyone can.

But, even with an abiding peace, continual effort and thoughtful intent are still necessary. It's easy to slip back into feelings of resentment, anger, fear, and angst. At times, dread enters my mind that tragedy will befall one of my loved ones again. At other times, I feel anger toward my fellow man for his blatant ignorance and hateful ways. And sometimes I feel a deep angst about life and the precarious balance that we strive to maintain. The sadness is still omnipresent, and it is often during times of great joy that it pervades. Inner peace needs to be continually renewed through processes that lead us to the divine presence, to God. In spite of all the turmoil, confusion, political upheaval, and suffering, my soul is healing and my heart has reopened itself to love and compassion, to newfound joy and abiding peace. For this, I am eternally grateful. Thank you, God, for your healing love, strength and courage. Let there be peace on earth, and let it begin with me.

Life is truly a mystery. We humans strive to understand all the complexities that abound; we endeavor to solve the mystery through the rational mind, scientific exploration, philosophy, and theology; we analyze, rationalize, and moralize; we purport, retort, and contort. But the mystery still retains vast secrets that may never be answered. After all, we are merely finite beings trying to grasp the infinite. The ego mind provides answers that can justify any action, right or wrong. But within each of us are the seeds of hope and the omnipotent power of the divine. God is within each of us. We are because God is.

Epilogue

Osama bin Laden is Dead: the Cycle of Violence Continues

On April 2, 2011, as I was preparing for the publication of this book, I received a text message from my son that Osama bin Laden had been killed by a team of Navy Seals. Ironically, we were at our cottage in Michigan, which we had purchased with Alicia's life insurance money in 2003 as a place to get away from all the craziness of war and the ongoing violence that was in the news daily.

The morning after hearing the news from our son we started receiving phone calls from the media asking for our thoughts and reactions to the breaking news. I had not had time to learn about the details of bin Laden's death, but I was made to feel the gravity of the situation while my emotions were still very raw. My first reaction was that the killing of bin Laden didn't really change a thing. My daughter and the others who perished on 9/11 were still dead; several hundred thousand innocent civilians in Afghanistan and Iraq, along with many thousands of soldiers who had died or been wounded as a result of our war on terror, would not be brought back to life or magically healed; a trillion-plus taxpayer dollars spent on war would still be gone; the devastation of two countries because of our war on terror would not be righted; the attack on our own country's moral integrity due to the atrocities of war and the willful torture of prisoners would not right itself; and the war on terror would go on as long as we continued fighting violence with more violence without addressing the underlying causes. I am vastly relieved that the evil of Osama bin Laden will not continue to destroy more innocent lives. But others will step forward to further his cause!

After Alicia was murdered I was asked what I would want to see happen to those responsible for her death. It was very clear to me and many other 9/11 families that these people needed to be brought to justice in an international court of law so that the whole world could see the face of justice and the evil behind these vicious acts of murder. After 9/11, much of the world responded with compassion to those of us in the United States. They voiced their allegiance to us in bringing those responsible to justice. I often wonder what would have resulted if we had chosen to combine our efforts with our allies, used our combined intelligence to find bin Laden and his followers, and not waged war on Afghanistan and then Iraq. Ironically, after all these years of war, in the end, Osama bin Laden was found as a result of intelligence gathering and a small team of highly trained specialists, not as a direct outcome of war.

As I began reading and listening to stories of bin Laden's killing, my emotions ranged from relief to anger, disappointment, sadness, and fear. When the news was announced, I witnessed Americans cheering outside of the White House and other public places; I read of people celebrating as if we had won a football game for a national title; I heard stories of crowds doing waves of cheers at baseball games. I was reminded of a time when many others around the world cheered after the attack on America that killed my daughter. I cannot find it within me to celebrate the killing of another human being. To me, this act was not justice! I fear that more people will die needlessly as a result of our actions as this self-perpetuating cycle of violence continues. Somehow, someday, this vicious cycle must stop, and we must find a better way, through greater understanding and deeper compassion, to get along with our fellow human beings. In the meantime, war rages on, the violence continues, and my heart is still deeply saddened. Peace is just a distant dream that someday will find its time, God willing.

Postscript

Peace Activities and Events after 9/11

The following is a partial list of the peace activities I have been involved in since Alicia's death, though some of the events and dates have eluded me. At the time, I didn't think to record them. Although the list is incomplete, it does demonstrate my commitment to and involvement in using my unique platform to effect change. Living in the Midwest and working full-time often precluded my full participation in events around the country and the world when opportunities arose. The following is a listing of the events and activities I was able to recall.

- *Organized a panel discussion of religious leaders from the Muslim, Christian, Jewish, Buddhist, Hindu and Quaker traditions to address issues around the September 11 attacks and discuss the related topics of faith, peace, justice, and forgiveness, Oct. 2001*

- *Presentation at Urbana University, Urbana, Ohio; hosted Gordon Judd, Vicar General, on conflict resolution, Sept. 2002*

- *Peace March, Iraq War protest – New York City, Feb. 15, 2003; first face to face meeting with Sept. 11 Families for Peaceful Tomorrows*

- *Kalamazoo Citizens for Peace, Keynote at Stetson Chapel on Kalamazoo College Campus, March 17, 2003*

- *Editorial for the Ann Arbor News – "Grieving Father Hopes for Peace," 3/23/03*

- *Documentary – "Critical Issues: Alternative Views," Kalamazoo, MI, March-May 2003*

- *September 11th Families for Peaceful Tomorrows' Stone Walk to create* awareness of the civilian casualties as a result of war, NYC; gave talks, interviews at a Chelsea church and in Union Square

- New York City Marathon participant; fundraiser for Alicia Titus Memorial Peace Fund, Nov. 2004

- Speech and workshop; served on organizing committee for the 7th Annual World Nonviolence Conference, Detroit, MI, April 20, 2005

- Article in The Messenger, a monthly journal of the Swedenborgian Church, Aug. 2002

- Speech at candlelight vigil in commemoration of the 60th anniversary of the bombings of Nagasaki and Hiroshima, Ann Arbor, MI, Aug. 8, 2005

- Speech at the Sunday morning service of the Department of Peace Conference in Washington D.C. along with Marianne Williamson, Sept. 11, 2005

- Presented to House of Representatives for the Department of Peace Bill introduction, Sept. 12, 2005

- Met with congressman from Michigan to talk about the Department of Peace Bill and peace and justice issues

- Speech at the University of Illinois along with Kathy Kelly (Voices in the Wilderness), AFSC, and Peaceful Tomorrows "Eyes Wide Open" display; served on a panel discussion with noted peacemakers, Sept. 16-17, 2005

- Marched at the Peace March with several hundred thousand peacemakers in Washington D.C. to protest the wars in Iraq and Afghanistan, Sept. 24, 2005

- Documentary, "Out of the Ordinary – Into the Extraordinary" on WMTV5 in Grosse Point, MI at the Grosse Point War Memorial, Dec. 7, 2005

- Keynote Speech at St. John's Episcopal Church in Worthington, OH for their Spring Retreat, April 2, 2006

- Presentation for the Department of Peace, St. John's Church, Worthington, OH, April 3, 2006

- Presented at the San Francisco Swedenborgian Church, 2006

- Keynote speech for the "Alleati per la Pace" Conference, Riccione, Italy, May 2006

- Presented and led discussions at Secondary Schools in Forli and Riccione, Italy, May 2006

- Discussed peace and justice issues with the Bishop of Forli Province, Italy, May 2006

- Newspaper and television interviews in Rimini, Italy, May 2006

- Workshop titled "Peacemaking in a Troubled World: How My Faith Informs My Commitment to Social Justice," Urbana University, Urbana, OH, Sept. 29, 2006

- Speech at The American Muslim Voice Conference, Newark, CA, Aug. 21, 2006

- Day of Remembrance Presentation, keynote by Marianne Williamson, presentations by Maria Mone from Ohio Dept. of Education and Professor Jim Boland, Wilmington College for Alicia Titus Memorial Peace series, Sept. 11, 2006

- Radio interview, Ann Arbor, MI, 107.7 FM, Sept. 19, 2006

- Speech, panel discussion with 9/11 families on war, peace, and justice held at the Ann Arbor Library in conjunction with the Magnum Photographs Display depicting the devastation of September 11, 2001, Sept. 20, 2006

- Keynote speech at North Dakota State University in Fargo, N.D. for World Peace Day Celebration, Jan. 21, 2007

- Speech at Wilmington College, Wilmington, OH, as a part of Religious Emphasis Week, public forum, classroom discussions, Feb. 7-8, 2007

- Speech at Ann Arbor Unitarian Universalist Church, public forum along with a former Marine who was in the Iraq invasion, 2007

- Made speech and hosted Bruce Wallace from 121 Project and Nisreen, a schoolteacher from Baghdad, Iraq for public forum on the devastation of war; interviewed by Dayton television and newspaper; presented in classrooms at Urbana University and Graham High School in Champaign Co., Ohio as a part of Alicia Titus Memorial Peace Series, Nov. 15-16, 2007

- Interviewed as part of a dissertation project on forgiveness, May 2008

- Keynote speech at World Focus Peace Conference at Churchill High School in Livonia, MI, March 28, 2009

- Interviews for newspapers from Australia and London (Guardian), San Francisco Chronicle, San Jose Mercury News, Detroit Free Press, Ann Arbor News, Columbus Dispatch, Springfield News and Sun, Urbana Daily Citizen, Dayton Daily News, Kalamazoo Gazette, and more

- Television interviews in Detroit, Dayton, Columbus, Rimini (Italy), and others

References

1 Project for the New American Century, Wikipedia.

2 Steps to Peace: The Journey of September Eleventh Families for Peaceful Tomorrows, Documentary, 2002.

3 Kushner, Robert S., When Bad Things Happen to Good People (Avon Books, 1983).

4 Swedenborg, Emanuel, True Christian Religion, Volume II (Boston and New York: Houghton Mifflin Co.; Cambridge: The Riverside Press), #466.

5 Swedenborg, Emanuel, Heaven and Hell (The Swedenborg Foundation, Inc., 1976).

6 Swedenborg, Emanuel, Divine Love and Wisdom (Boston and New York: Houghton Mifflin Co.).

7 Washington, James M., The Essential Writings and Speeches of Martin Luther King (Harper Collins Publishers, New York), 594.

8 www.peacefultomorrrows.org. Mission statement and activities.

9 McNamara, Robert S. and Blight, James G., Wilson's Ghost (New York: Public Affairs, 2001).

10 Swedenborg, Emanuel, Heaven and Hell (Boston and New York: Houghton and Mifflin Company).

11 Elliot, Michael, "They Had A Plan," Time, August 12, 2002.

12 Ibid.

13 Ahmed, Nafeez Mosaddeq, The War on Freedom: How and Why America was Attacked—September 11, 2001 (Tree of Life Publications, 2002).

14 Williamson, Marianne, Speech at the Department of Peace Conference, Washington D.C., September 11, 2005.

15 Van Dusen, Wilson, Uses: A Way of Personal and Spiritual Growth (New York: The Swedenborg Foundation, Inc., 1981).

16 Swedenborg, Emanuel, Divine Love and Wisdom (Boston and New York: Houghton Mifflin Co).

About the Author

John Titus is a retired college administrator and mental health counselor who divides his time between Michigan and Ohio. He is a devoted husband, father and grandfather and important to this book is the father of Alicia Nicole Titus, who was violently murdered while working as a flight attendant on United Airlines flight 175 on September 11, 2001. Since Alicia's death, John has become a strong advocate for peace and social justice, writing articles, doing documentaries, political activism and giving talks all over the United States, Canada and Italy on these and related issues. In his efforts to bring about a more peaceful and just world he has spoken at universities, colleges, churches, the American Muslim Voice Convention, the Department of Peace Conference, at a congressional committee to reintroduce the Department of Peace Bill, the Alleati per la Pace conference in Riccione, Italy and the Global Nonviolence Conference to name a few. He has joined with other peace organizations such as the Interfaith Council for Peace and Justice, Veterans for Peace, the National Peace Academy and the The National Peace Alliance along with others. He is a current member and former steering committee member of September 11th Families for Peaceful Tomorrows, an organization of 9/11 victim's family members and friends who officially formed in February of 2002 to speak out on the atrocities of war, especially civilian casualties, to promote transparency in government decisions about the 9/11 attack, to encourage alternatives to war and to further efforts towards peace and justice throughout the world.